PROFESSIONAL ETHICS IN EDUCATION SERIES

Kenneth A. Strike, Editor

The Ethics of School Administration
Kenneth A. Strike, Emil J. Haller
and Jonas F. Soltis

Classroom Life as Civic Education:
Individual Achievement and Student Cooperation in Schools
David C. Bricker

The Ethics of Special Education
Kenneth R. Howe
and Ofelia B. Miramontes

The Ethics of Special Education

Kenneth R. Howe
and
Ofelia B. Miramontes

Teachers College, Columbia University
New York and London

Published by Teachers College Press, 1234 Amsterdam Avenue
New York, NY 10027

Library of Congress Cataloging-in-Publication Data

Howe. Kenneth Ross.
The ethics of special education / Kenneth R. Howe, Ofelia B. Miramontes.
p. cm.—(Professional ethics in education series)
Includes bibliographical references and index.
ISBN 0-8077-3179-X
1. Special education—United States—Moral and ethical aspects—Case studies. I. Miramontes, Ofelia B. II. Title. III. Series.
LC3981.H68 1992
174'93719'0973—dc20 92-8434

ISBN 0-8077-3179-X (pbk.)

Printed on acid-free paper

Manufactured in the United States of America

09 08 07 06 05 04 03 02 01 8 7 6 5 4

To Tonda, just for being
the constant breath of fresh air she is;

and to Bill
for his love, support, and enduring struggle
to lead an ethical life.

Contents

Foreword

A common misperception is that the profession of special education is a haven for those of us who want to be reassured that we are doing the right thing, that in nearly all cases we know what is right and need only the commitment to do what our policies or values tell us. This misperception is perpetuated, I suspect, by the observation that we are advocates for students with whom most teachers have not been anxious to work and by our avowal of high moral purpose—the achievement of justice, equal opportunity, and social acceptance, for example. In fact, we special educators are engaged in an enterprise that is by nature particularly chancy. Our primary objective is the accommodation of the extremes of human diversity, by creating variations in educational structures to modulate outcomes for the benefit of individual students, a task with often unpredictable demands and consequences.

We face especially difficult ethical decisions because we deal with the most unusual exceptions to the rule. The theory and practice of special education are derived from a fundamental distrust of apparently "safe" generalizations that hold for the vast majority of cases. When teachers or policy makers use the phrase "all children," for example, we necessarily ask whether "all" is to be taken literally. When someone asserts that a program is "the right thing to do," we ask why it is said to be right and whether it is right in all cases. This book challenges all of us to think more carefully about the questions we ask and how we formulate our answers.

Educators of nearly every description should be interested in this book. Few, if any, can escape all of the difficult decisions that confront special educators. Most exceptional children and youth are taught in regular schools, and most are found in ordinary classrooms for at least part of the school day. Furthermore, the boundaries between special and general education are blurred by both the nature of students' differences and the nature of the structures we devise to accommodate them. In many ways, if not in most, the ethical quandaries of general educators parallel those of special educators, and we encounter these ethical predicaments in every area of our endeavors.

Whether we are teaching exceptional students, preparing special education teachers, preparing to become a teacher of exceptional students, administering special education programs, or doing research in special education, the nature of our task frequently prompts all of us—though not always successfully—to consider the ethical implications of our decisions about students with exceptionalities. A case in point that nearly every student and faculty member in higher education has encountered is how to respond to the teacher in training who has an emotional or behavioral disorder (see McGee & Kauffman, 1989). How do we balance our responsibility to the teacher in training with our responsibility to children? How do we determine what is the right thing to do when we must consider at once the individual's personal and professional future, his or her rights to accommodation, and the risk to the youngsters she or he might teach—and do so with attention to the ethics of confidentiality, due process, and professional relationships?

Howe and Miramontes note that education, and especially special education, is rife with ethical problems. This is no overstatement, as nearly any beginning special education teacher can tell you. How should I respond, a beginning teacher asked us recently, when I go into an eligibility meeting having been told by the school psychologist that the placement decision has, in effect, already been made? What should I do, another teacher wondered, when an administrator's program description misrepresents to a parent what will actually be provided to her child? Teachers routinely face dilemmas in dealing with students whose extreme needs other individuals choose to ignore, with education—general or special—that is clearly stultifying, and with students who have been misplaced in special programs. A teacher of children with serious emotional and behavioral disorders wrote to me this year about her frustrations:

> We have been warned that disciplinary letters may be placed in our files if we don't complete evaluation and placement of newly referred kids within 30 days of obtaining their parents' signature. Nobody can tell me how to teach 40 kids and still have time to do testing.

Her circumstance is hauntingly like that described by Katzen (1980) more than a decade ago, and it should remind us of the ethical questions raised by telling teachers (or anyone else) that they ought to do what they can't. She goes on to describe problems involving other social agencies:

> A kindergarten boy killed the classroom hamster in front of the entire class and then delivered a sermon on the hamster's great

> happiness at being with Jesus now. He also told us repeatedly that he planned to kill himself so that he could be happier. (He did have access to guns and poisons.) His violent behaviors, if unchecked, occurred at an average rate of 6 per minute and included hitting, biting, stabbing, kicking, strangling, burning, and more. I tried desperately to find residential treatment for this child. There is no facility for him in ______, and the district refused to pay for sending him to ______. He never received any counselling. By threatening to quit my job and explaining liability problems if a child in his class was seriously hurt, I did get an aide for him. . . .

The ethical dilemmas this teacher faced are common for special educators. Unfortunately, special education training programs regarding collegial relationships, research projects, and policy making processes have given only superficial attention to how we might best resolve our ethical problems. For far too long we have looked only to policy and dogma to guide our decisions. *The Ethics of Special Education* will help us think more deeply and clearly about the nature of our dilemmas and our alternative courses of action.

As special educators, we are beset by seemingly intractable questions and conflicts. The questions seem intractable in part, I suppose, because we view them as policy issues. Policies are attempts to constrain the boundaries of decision making, to limit the ways in which we are allowed to make decisions. Policies seem made to be broken, however, because they can seldom, if ever, be written to cover all contingencies. We frequently find that policies are inadequate guides to action in the individual case; they often fail to address circumstances that from our personal vantage point are pivotal for making an ethical decision.

When an apparently good policy, perhaps even a law, tells us to do something that our knowledge of the individual case tells us is wrong, what is the right thing to do? Consider the problem of deciding who should receive special services. Special education, like other social services, typically has eligibility criteria and procedures—policies—intended to prevent unrestricted access from bankrupting the program, to ensure the availability of services to students most in need, and to reduce capricious labeling and needless stigma. If we find that a student needs special services yet does not meet the eligibility criteria for those services, and appropriate services are not available elsewhere, what should we do—deny the services or "fudge" the eligibility policy? We are faced with an ethical dilemma; we must try to determine which is the lesser of two evils. Such dilemmas force us to consider the limits of policy in regulating decisions and to see that ethical deliberation must include attention to specific circumstances and personal moral values.

Questions about special education may also seem intractable because people have seemingly irresolvable differences in the criteria they consider most important in the individual case; one person's preferred perspective is another's view of perdition. Given the recognition that mental retardation exists, how do we determine that a student has it? How much weight should we give to intelligence tests in determining that a student has mental retardation? Is someone's personal judgment (perhaps it could be called "expert," "clinical," or "subjective") preferable to a standardized test of intelligence (which, one might argue, is "biased," "inappropriately normed," or "invalid")? Whose clinical judgment should we trust? Whose moral philosophy should guide us? Policy has its limitations, as we have seen, but its absence leaves us vulnerable to dangerously changeable currents of personal power and charisma.

Given the difficulty of ethical decision making, it is easy to understand the lure of method and creed as templates for drawing conclusions. We prize the simplicity and ostensible certainty of a rule book or a moral authority. It is easier—and to some it feels "safer"—to let others do our thinking for us. Howe and Miramontes do not tell us how we should resolve our ethical dilemmas, but they do help us understand how we might construct our own resolutions without falling prey to the temptation to oversimplify the ethical questions we ask or the answers we offer.

Ethical problems and the way we think about them are often revealed in our discussions of the issue of mainstreaming, integration, or inclusion. A couple of doctoral students and I, watching a video called *Regular lives* (Goodwin & Wurzburg, 1987), were struck by the closing commentary on the practice of including all students with disabilities in ordinary schools and classrooms:

> It really doesn't matter whether or not it works. It does work, and that's great. But even if it didn't work it would still be the thing to do, because it's right. It's treating people with dignity. It's caring about people and letting people know that they're worthwhile humans.

At the moment we punched the VCR's rewind button, actor Wilford Brimley appeared on a regular commercial channel, hawking instant oatmeal. "It's the right thing to do," he advised with great sincerity. The humor of this entirely fortuitous event was not lost on us, but our burst of laughter was followed by the saddening realization that much of the advocacy in our field is painfully close to advertising "hype," unsettlingly like the deceptive "sound bite" that makes a politician's chicanery attractive to voters. We understood that "right" has clear ethical connotations as used by the speaker in *Regular lives*; its ethical meaning as used by Wilford Brimley is, at best, obscure. Nevertheless, this juxtaposition of statements about "rightness" prompted us to think more about what is "right" about inclusion.

The speaker in *Regular lives* gives us few clues about what she means by "it works." Presumably, however, "it works" means that full inclusion of all students provides greater benefits than any available alternative. We might then inquire whether her statement that "it works" applies to any case, to most cases, or to all cases. The distinctions among these possibilities—any, most, and all—are critical in guiding the practice of special education and understanding the ethics of our decisions. Our knowledge of the research literature, and our personal experiences as well, informed us that inclusion in regular schools and classes clearly "works" for many students, perhaps for most, but obviously not for all. Under what conditions, if any, is an approach to education (or to child discipline, medical treatment, or any other human service) "right" even if it doesn't "work?" Can education or treatment be morally "right" if it provides no benefit, even if it does harm? Are we to assume that what is "right" for most students is "right" for all, regardless of benefit or harm in the individual case?

We wondered whether the speaker in *Regular lives* might be suggesting that including students with disabilities in regular schools and classrooms is the only possible way to treat them with dignity, to care about them, and to let them know that they're worthwhile humans; therefore, alternatives to inclusion can not be "right," even if they offer other benefits. Could she be suggesting that alternatives to inclusion in regular schools and classrooms are inherently wrong for all students because none permits us to treat any student with dignity, to demonstrate caring, or to show students that they are worthwhile human beings? We had seen other assertions that no alternative to such inclusion either "works" or is compatible with dignity, caring, and expression of respect for students (e.g., Lipsky & Gartner, 1987, 1991). Again, the research and professional literatures and our own experiences told us something contrary—that alternatives to inclusion do "work" for some students and that dignity, caring, and expressions of students' value as human beings have in many cases been prominent features of these alternatives. How far can a generalization about what "works" and what is "right" be stretched, we wondered, without its becoming prevarication? How do we weigh the ethical implications of an overgeneralization, particularly in a field of study and practice having as its conceptual and moral cornerstone the repudiation of overgeneralizations about children and their education?

We put another tape into the VCR, this time *Asylum* (Patton, Mondale, & Monmaney, 1988), an examination of residential institutions for persons with mental illness, focusing on St. Elizabeth's Hospital in Washington, DC as an example. It features pro and con arguments on the deinstitutionalization movement, portraying both the horrors of abuse in institutions and the benefits of humane institutional care. The video shows both the successes and the failures of alternatives to institutions; it neither degrades the value of community-based treatment alternatives for many individuals, nor does it hide the failure of community alternatives for many others. Reflecting on the humanitarian crusade of Dorothea Dix in the mid nineteenth century to remove the mentally ill from jails and almshouses and place them in the institutions which humanitarian crusaders of the mid twentieth century sought to close, the narrator concludes:

> It seems we have come full circle since the days of Dorothea Dix. Where she saw mentally ill paupers locked in jails, we find them trapped on the streets. Today, the struggle remains what it was for Dix—to treat the afflicted in a way that does more good than harm, and to offer the needy, at the very least, shelter. No one wants to go back to the asylums of old, but it should be possible to salvage what was good about the place. It was warmer than a jail, safer to sleep in than an alley; it stood for our desire to heal the disturbed. Now, much of it lies in ruins. And yet we have not really created or built or even dreamed of anything to take the place of the asylum.

As the story of St. Elizabeth's and the institutionalization and deinstitutionalization movements unwound, we saw unmistakable parallels between the movement to depopulate institutions and the current movement to empty special schools and classes. We were impressed by *Asylum's* closing commentary, which cautions against the overgeneralization that alternatives to institutional care are always "right" and suggests that preservation of the asylum in its best sense may be a "right" course of action, in that it will serve the needs of some individuals better than any alternative we know.

I have long felt that we give too little thought to ethical dilemmas in special education. Like other groups in our society today, we special educators find simplistic answers to complex problems highly seductive. Too often, we offer or accept oversimplified responses to ethical issues: "It's right because it's the law," "It's right because it's consistent with our concept of human dignity," "It's wrong because it separates out and segregates," "It's right because it works in most cases," "It's wrong because it does not work for all," and so on. Viewing *Regular lives* and *Asylum* with my two students and pondering the ethical questions they raised highlighted for me once again the need for a volume like this one.

Neither we who work in higher education nor our students nor professionals providing direct services to children and youth have had an accessible guide to ethical deliberation in special education. When I reviewed a paper on this topic by Howe and Miramontes (1991), I immediately hoped that the authors would prepare a book-length manuscript. I am grateful to them, as I am sure my colleagues and students will be, for writing this sorely needed resource for special education students and professionals. This book will, I am confident, do much to raise the level of our thinking about ethical issues and, ultimately, the quality of the difficult decisions we make. It will do so because it provides a framework for reflection and deliberation rather than a set of prescriptions. By using a case-based approach in which they sketch common dilemmas to which only the most doctrinaire or legalistic can give pat answers, Howe and Miramontes give us vivid lessons in what it means to take the ethics of our profession seriously.

James M. Kauffman
The University of Virginia

REFERENCES

Goodwin, T., & Wurzburg, G. (Producers and Directors). (1987). *Regular lives.* [Video Cassette]. Syracuse, NY: Syracuse University.

Howe, K., & Miramontes, O. (1991). A framework for ethical deliberation in special education. *Journal of Special Education, 25*, 7–25.

Katzen, K. (1980). A teacher's view. *Exceptional Children, 48*, 582.

Lipsky, D., & Gartner, A. (1987). Capable of achievement and worthy of respect: Education for handicapped students as if they were full-fledged human beings. *Exceptional Children, 54*, 69–74.

Lipsky, D., & Gartner, A. (1991). Restructuring for quality. In J. Lloyd, A. Repp, & N. Singh (Eds.), *The regular education initiative: Alternative perspectives on concepts, issues, and models* (pp. 43–57). Sycamore, IL: Sycamore.

McGee, K., & Kauffman, J. (1989). Educating teachers with emotional disabilities: A balance of private and public interests. *Teacher Education and Special Education, 12*(3), 110–116.

Patton, S. (Producer), Mondale, S. (Director), & Monmaney, T. (Writer). (1988). *Asylum.* [Video Cassette]. Washington, DC: Stone Lantern Films.

A Note to the Instructor

This book is not an exercise in "applied ethics," if such a description assumes that ethical deliberation should proceed by having experts supply theory that is then to be applied to specific ethically problematic situations in order to categorize and "solve" them. Instead, it is an exercise in prompting a brand of ethical reflection that is able to identify and make use of whatever considerations are relevant and helpful. Our position, which is by no means unusual today, is that the key to fostering effective ethical deliberation is practice in reasoning and collaborating about ethically problematic situations, not mere mastery of a given set of principles and precepts.

This orientation to the teaching of ethics goes a long way toward explaining the case-based approach of this book. We by no means exclude or disparage ethical theory. On the other hand, we set out to consistently make it do some work, as well as to lay bare its limits vis-à-vis real-world ethical problems. Accordingly, each discussion this book contains, no matter how abstract and theoretical, is couched in terms of an ethically problematic situation that grows out of the institution and practice of special education.

Regarding the audience for this book, we direct our conversations to special educators, and particularly to their peculiar predicaments and obligations. However, because educational administrators at all levels, school psychologists, and regular education teachers invariably play key roles in, and thus cannot avoid being a part of, the kinds of ethically problematic policies and situations we describe, we believe that this book should prove valuable to instructors of teachers and of educational administrators of all types.

Regarding pedagogy, we actively discourage the "applied ethics" model alluded to above. Instructors and students alike are encouraged to use the theory and concepts introduced throughout the book as appropriate, *but only as appropriate*. We will have more to say about what this amounts to in Chapters 1 and 2, but it is worth emphasizing here that the ethical theories we introduce are not immune from criticism, nor is our particular treatment of them. Furthermore, it is a mistake, in our estimation, to proceed on the assumption that given ethical problems can always be effectively approached by plugging them into this or that theoretical framework and neatly deducing a solution—the world is just too messy for that. We encourage instructors and students to employ theoretical principles and concepts as tools that are often quite valuable for identifying issues and suggesting solutions, but to also maintain confidence in their own judgment about how best to approach given problems.

By its very nature, this book requires using some form of the case method. Beyond this, we have several further suggestions. Chapters 3 to 5 provide numerous cases, accompanied by our analyses. The latter present examples of ferreting out issues and reasoning toward some policy or action. Students should be encouraged to take these analyses as points of departure and to agree, disagree, or modify the positions advanced on the basis of their own reflections. These cases and analyses may be used in conjunction with and as preparation for the cases in Appendix A, which have no accompanying analyses, and a variant of the teaching method about to be described may be fruitfully employed.

First, it is advisable to require students to think hard about a given case before it is considered in class. In our teaching, we require students to come to class with a prepared case analysis that includes the following elements: (1) an enumeration of the reasonable alternatives, (2) an endorsement of one of the alternatives, (3) a brief sketch of the reasons that support the alternative endorsed over the alternatives rejected, and (4) a consideration of any important missing information that, if available, could alter the judgment made. (Because of the possibility that not all the information needed is presented in a particular case—a bugaboo of paper cases—some device is needed to prevent this problem from bringing discussion to a full stop.)

Second, we typically divide students into groups of from five to seven and give them roughly half an hour to come up with some joint deliberation in terms of the four-part framework above, allowing that there might be dissenters. Following this, we ask three groups, one at a time, to present their findings to the whole group (in our experience three groups exhaust the competing views and considerations) and then have a whole-group discussion. We press for consensus, but often settle for having articulated several competing, but well-considered, views.

Third, establishing an open but critical climate is essential to an effective exploration of the issues raised. It is frequently an unfamiliar (and at times uncomfortable) experience for individuals to explore strongly held but often unexamined beliefs in a public forum. Analysis and understanding will be enhanced by frank discussion of the issues.

Finally, we strongly endorse team teaching that includes a philosopher and an expert in special education. Although we have rarely been able to enjoy this luxury ourselves, our collaboration on this book has shown us how exceedingly valuable having two sets of tools and concerns can be.

Acknowledgments

The idea for this book began with the discovery of a shared interest in the ethics of special education that emerged fortuitously during casual conversation. This idea quickly began to unfold, and we are indebted to Kenneth Strike, editor of the Professional Ethics in Education series, for his receptiveness to our incipient idea as well as for his subsequent willingness to review our prospectus, to suggest improvements, and to recommend it to Teachers College Press. At the Press we thank Sarah Biondello, Brian Ellerbeck, Carol Collins, and Cynthia Fairbanks for their valuable suggestions regarding the organization of the book and for their roles in guiding it to completion.

The book would not have been possible without the help of numerous individuals who supplied us with the ideas for the cases upon which the book so heavily depends. These individuals include students in past sections of our social foundations, teacher ethics, and special education courses. We especially thank several clinical faculty members in the Partners in Education program at the University of Colorado at Boulder who not only inspired cases but also spent hours discussing with us the ethical dimensions of their workaday lives as special educators in the public schools. They are Kathy Padilla, Denise Kale, Jerry Ohrt, and Tonda Potts. The Spencer Foundation also should be acknowledged for the support it provided to Kenneth Howe through its postdoctoral fellowship program. This support was particularly instrumental in the preparation of Chapter 3.

Finally, we thank James Kauffman for generously agreeing to write the Foreword.

CHAPTER 1

Introduction

Education is rife with ethical problems—problems concerning how to treat individual students, how to ensure equal educational opportunity for all, how to respect the views of parents, how to deal with colleagues, and how to do all these things while maintaining one's personal integrity and allegiance to the practice of education. Such problems are often magnified within special education, for at least two reasons. First, the burgeoning of special education in the last several decades developed largely out of an awakened commitment to the ethical requirement that all individuals should be provided with access to a decent public education, regardless of how they might differ from the general population with respect to various skills, abilities, and powers that affect school performance. Thus, special education has a particularly strong ethical mission, and decisions made through the special education process have lifelong ramifications for individuals. Second, because special education is indeed "special" it taxes the traditional organizational structure and resources of schools, as well as the knowledge and skills of teachers. Integration is perhaps the most widespread and familiar example of the ethical challenges raised by special education.

Despite the ethical quagmires that special education engenders, it is probably safe to say that the ethics of special education has so far received scant attention, either as a field of ethical inquiry or as a topic in teacher education. Accordingly, this book has both theoretical and pedagogical aims. At a theoretical level, it will seek to define the kinds of problems that go into making up the "ethics of special education," as well as to suggest the kinds of perspectives—from the law and moral philosophy—that go into establishing a general framework for ethical deliberation about such problems. At a pedagogical level, it will seek to provide students with practice, both individual and collaborative, in grappling with the ethical problems that are endemic to special education. Although the two levels are related in intimate ways, the pedagogical level will be emphasized, consistent with the general aims of the "Professional Ethics in Education Series."

A PRELIMINARY OBSERVATION REGARDING THE STUDY OF ETHICS

It will be useful to include at the outset a few general remarks about the scope and limits of the study of ethics. According to Benjamin and Curtis (1986), ethical deliberation is concerned with answering the following question: "What, *all things considered*, ought to be done in a given situation?" (p. 9). The nature of this question helps to distinguish ethical deliberation from certain other intellectual activities. For example, unlike the reasonably well-defined puzzle solving that characterizes mathematics and physics, ethical deliberation must take into account an almost boundless array of considerations, including the facts and the law, as well as personal beliefs, attachments, feelings, and conceptions of the good life. This renders ethical deliberation exceedingly complex, uncertain, and tentative. Furthermore, and also unlike the problem solving of mathematics and physics, everyone, not just the experts, faces ethical problems. Accordingly, everyone is (or should be) afforded a voice and possesses a form of expertise when it comes to ethical deliberation. This renders ethical deliberation often personal, or "subjective."

The complex, uncertain, tentative, and subjective features of ethical deliberation too often encourage ethical skepticism—the view that there are "no right answers," that "ethics is just all a matter of opinion." Rather than trying to meet skepticism head on, we trust it will simply fall by the wayside as this book unfolds. We believe that the value of reflecting on how to recognize and weigh the considerations that go into ethical deliberation will reveal itself over the course of considering ethically problematic situations, and that a clearer understanding of the limitations, as well as the promise, of careful thought about ethical issues in special education will naturally emerge. In place of skepticism we urge the reader to set his or her sights on the right target for the study of ethics by heeding Aristotle's famous advice: "Our treatment will be adequate if we make it as precise as the subject matter allows" (in Bambrough, 1963, p. 287).

ORGANIZATION OF THE BOOK

The book consists of six chapters. Chapter 2 is primarily devoted to general theoretical concerns. It tackles the question of the nature of ethical deliberation in terms of the law, facts and values, and moral philosophy, and it sets the stage for the remaining chapters. Moral philosophy is emphasized and is treated in terms of the degree of abstraction of deliberation—ranging from problems of national policy to face-to-face ethical problems involving teachers, students, and parents. These two end points are identified with "principle-based" and "virtue-based" moral theories, respectively. The chapter concludes by noting that teachers are often caught between these two end points by virtue of their "role-related obligations." In a slightly different way, schools and school districts are caught between these two perspectives by virtue of their obligations to given communities.

Chapters 3 through 5 are framed in terms of ethically problematic cases that illustrate more general ethical issues in special education. The cases originate from a variety of sources: personal experience; conversations with practicing special education teachers and administrators; a collaborative research project on teacher ethics with classroom teachers, administrators, and staff developers; student assignments in graduate courses in special education; and fictionalized versions of celebrated legal cases.

Our general approach in Chapters 3 through 5 is to provide a brief discussion of a general issue, for instance, "labeling"; illustrate it in terms of a case; and then provide a discussion of the case. The case study approach is especially appropriate, in our estimation, because deliberating about real-life cases is the most effective way to provide practice in employing the social and intellectual skills required for effective ethical deliberation (see, for example, Jonsen & Toulmin, 1988; Strike & Soltis, 1985; and Howe, 1986). In the discussions provided we invariably take a position. By doing so, we hope to provide examples of what reasonably careful and comprehensive analyses look like—analyses that terminate with some action that is to be taken. On the other hand, our aim is limited to getting the deliberative ball rolling in a way that invites reasoned deliberation. Thus, we do not attempt to provide unassailable solutions, nor do we pursue the cases in such detail that further discussion and reasoned disagreement is inhibited.

The general themes of Chapters 3 through 5 are "Public Policy and the Mission of Special Education," "Institutional Demands and Constraints," and "Students and Parents as Sources of Obligation," respectively. These three themes correspond to the positions in which teachers find themselves vis-à-vis the concreteness of the ethical problems they face. "Public Policy and the Mission of Special Education" concerns issues in which teachers' deliberations are least personal and least likely to have immediate effects (for example, whether to support a given piece of special education legislation). In contrast, "Students and Parents as Sources of Obligation" concerns issues in which teachers' involvement is most personal and most likely to have direct effects on students and parents (for instance, whether to maintain a student's confidentiality). Between these two extremes, "Institutional Demands and Constraints" concerns issues in which teachers are caught between local policy on the one hand and students and parents they personally know on the other (such as whether their particular school should spend more on special or gifted education).

Chapters 3 through 5 represent a progression from the most abstract and impersonal to the most concrete and personal kinds of issues. Although we have some worries about starting with issues farthest removed from day-to-day practice, our rationale for proceeding in this way is that it enables the discussion of cases to unfold in such a way that the context in which the problems are set becomes progressively more focused on the features of situations over which individuals have some personal and immediate control. General questions of law and policy form part of the background for the more concrete problems at the institutional level, and, in turn, these general policy and institutional issues form part of the background for the even more concrete problems at the level of personal relationships with parents and students. Ethical discussions can quickly reach an impasse if individuals throw up their hands, claiming there is nothing they can do because the problem is with a law or policy or with institutional constraints over which they have no control. The law, policy, and institutional constraints are indeed often the source of problems, and for this reason they should be examined, evaluated, and, where necessary, changed. On the other hand, the fact that these things are difficult to change (at least quickly enough to have an impact on a situation that calls for immediate attention) in no way eliminates the need for ethical deliberation. On the contrary, as intimated above, they are important background features of the concrete ethical problems with which individuals must contend.

One final remark about the nature of these three chapters is in order. The collection of cases was constructed to meet two aims. First, the cases in each of these chapters are designed to coincide with the general theme of the chapter. Thus, the cases are written with the intent to depict a policy issue, an institutional issue, or a more personal issue. As it turns out, in the real world of practice actual cases often (if not always) have all three elements, and which one is most important to consider is simply a matter of emphasis and interest. Second, and sometimes competing with the first aim, the collection of cases is intended to capture the most important and frequently occurring ethical problems that special education presents.

Chapter 6 concludes the book, providing a brief discussion of the ethics of compromise and taking a second look at several cases from the preceding chapters in terms of this issue.

GETTING STARTED

By way of an initiation into the method of case studies, and to help set the stage for the discussion in Chapter 2, consider the following case and the questions that follow. (In Chapter 2 we will explore the questions raised by this case in some depth.)

Case: Where are the Lines to be Drawn?

Amy Rowley was a hearing impaired first grader. Consistent with the requirements of the Education for All Handicapped Children Act (P.L. 94–142), an individualized educational program (IEP) was devised for Amy that provided her with a hearing aid and instruction in sign language and lip reading. Against the protests of Amy's parents, however, the district special education office refused to provide an interpreter for Amy to translate spoken language in the classroom. The district reasoned that because Amy "was achieving educationally, academically, and socially" (she was above average in each case) and was "a remarkably well-adjusted child," it had no obligation to try to improve her performance further. The district also worried about a snowball effect, in which all sorts of demands would be made by parents, causing a political and budgetary crisis.

Amy's parents rejected the reasoning of the district. In their view, Amy was being denied an equal educational opportunity because they believed if she was provided with an interpreter, she would be able to do much better academically. In the language of the Rowleys's attorneys, not providing Amy with an interpreter denied her the opportunity to "maximize her potential commensurate with the opportunity provided to other children." How much good an interpreter would do was disputed by the district.

Two positions emerged within the school that Amy attended: The school principal and a slight majority of the regular classroom teachers sided with the Rowleys; the remainder of the teachers and the special education resource teacher sided with the district and the special education office.

- How is the law relevant to cases such as Amy Rowley's?
- Do you think the law should support the Rowleys?
- What factual information is relevant to this case?
- How does one set of facts rather than another lead to a different conclusion?
- What ethical principles are involved in this case?
- Are any principles in conflict?
- Should whether one is a parent, regular classroom teacher, special education teacher, or administrator affect the position that one supports?
- Finally, what position would you support, *all things considered*?

CHAPTER 2

The Nature of Ethical Deliberation

The aim of this chapter is to provide a discussion of the general kinds of issues that may be used to frame the ethics of special education. In particular, we will examine ethical deliberation in terms of law and ethics, the fact–value distinction, and moral philosophy. As we stated in Chapter 1, this chapter will be relatively theoretical and abstract in nature. Unlike the chapters to follow, the emphasis will be largely on the exposition of issues rather than on grappling with ethically problematic cases. Our strategy throughout this chapter will be to raise and delineate issues rather than to take firm stands.

We ended the previous chapter with the case of Amy Rowley. It is a slightly fictionalized version of an actual case (*Rowley* v. *Board of Education*) that was decided by the U.S. Supreme Court in 1982. Before proceeding, a brief continuation of the case is in order.

Case: Where Are the Lines to Be Drawn? (continued)

The Rowleys ultimately sued to obtain an interpreter for Amy and a lower court decided in their favor. However, the Supreme Court overturned the lower court, resting its reasoning largely on how Congress intended the expression "free appropriate education," mandated by P.L. 94–142, to be interpreted. The Court decided that Congress intended no "substantive educational standard" by this expression and, in particular, that it did not intend the standard to be "strict equality of opportunity or services" or "maximizing potential." It also cited the evidence that Amy "was achieving educationally, academically, and socially," and that she "was a remarkably well-adjusted child" as evidence that she was receiving a "benefit," as mandated by P.L. 94–142. (The *Rowley* case is described in Strahan & Turner, 1987, pp. 22–34).

We now turn to our detailed discussions of the law and ethics, the fact/value distinction, and moral philosophy. At the end of such discussion we will again ask the reader to ponder questions that relate to the *Rowley* case, but this time in light of the complexities we introduce.

LAW AND ETHICS

The federal courts, regulatory agencies, and Congress have so thoroughly insinuated themselves into various aspects of special education that there is a danger that ethical questions will be ignored in favor of legal ones. We do not mean to suggest that law and ethics are completely distinct. On the contrary, law and ethics are intimately related, insofar as laws frequently encompass ethical principles and insofar as a *prima facie* ethical obligation exists to obey the law. On the other hand, the overlap of law and ethics does not imply that they perfectly coincide, for the ethical principles encompassed may be objectionable and *prima facie* obligations may therefore need to be overridden. For example, Martin Luther King Jr.'s justification for breaking Jim Crow laws was ethical: He didn't claim that laws that sanctioned racial discrimination did not exist or that they were not legally binding; he claimed instead that they should be disobeyed because they were unjust. In a similar vein, the Rowleys themselves would have to acknowledge that the Supreme Court's decision was legally binding, though they would not thereby be required to acknowledge that it was ethically correct. In general, then, whether a law is ethical and whether it is legally binding are distinguishable.

Another way to distinguish law and ethics is captured by the description of the law as a "blunt instrument." What this means is that the law cannot take into account all the intricacies that characterize concrete ethical judgments. For example, most people would think it was unethical for an individual to make promises he or she didn't intend to keep in order to win sexual favors. But imagine how ineffective it would be to try to prevent this sort of behavior by enacting a general legal prohibition against lying. In order for laws to work in the sense of commanding citizens' attention and respect, they must be reasonably enforceable. Furthermore, for citizens to know what is legally required of them, the law must be reasonably free of distinctions between one situation and another that are so fine that citizens have no idea what they are permitted to do. For both of these reasons—to be enforceable and to be informative to citizens—the law must be relatively general in nature, relatively "blunt."

However, occasions frequently arise in which a particular law must be sharpened, because it is too blunt to provide sufficient guidance in a specific problematic case. To switch metaphors, the law possesses an "open texture" (Hart, 1961) that sometimes needs to be filled in. In the *Rowley* case, for instance, the Court had to interpret the open-textured expression "free appropriate education"; it also had to determine whether the "maximizing potential" criterion, introduced by the Rowleys's attorneys, should be the criterion of equality of educational opportunity. Because there is no way to simply inspect the wording of P.L. 94–142 and deduce how to interpret these expressions, the Court had to fill in the open texture using its own best judgment. Furthermore, the Court filled in the open texture by making an ethical judgment. In particular, "maximizing potential" is one way that the ethical principle of equality of educational opportunity might be interpreted (equal access and equal outcomes are examples of others), and the Court rejected this interpretation. Indeed, the Court may have rejected the principle of equal educational opportunity in the context of P.L. 94–142 altogether. But regardless of how one characterizes the Court's decision or judges its merits, the important point is this: It had a significant ethical dimension.

In summary, the relationship between law and ethics may be characterized in four ways. First, existing laws may be subject to ethical criticism based on ethical principles external to the laws in question. Second, laws are by nature relatively general and neither capture the whole of ethics nor eliminate the need for ethical deliberation. Third, the open texture of the law leaves room for interpretation, and the interpretations employed often have ethical content. Fourth, even where interpretation is not required, where the law is settled, it nonetheless presupposes ethical commitments.

What these features of the law imply is that although the law and ethics cannot be totally separated, neither can they be reduced to one another. In most cases, the legal thing to do will also be the ethical thing to do. But this will not always be so, since laws and regulations may be defective from an ethical point of view. Furthermore, since laws and regulations are unavoidably general and open-textured, particular cases frequently require ethical deliberation to fill in the gaps.

Do you agree with the Supreme Court's reasoning in the *Rowley* case? If not, why not?

FACTS AND VALUES

Consider the general ethical principle, "Don't harm others *without good reason*." Although it is doubtful that anyone would seriously challenge this principle, it can nonetheless be difficult to apply. For even when people agree on the principle, they can disagree on how the *good reason* clause is to be interpreted in light of the facts. Thus, what at first appears to be a disagreement about ethical principles can turn out to be a disagreement about the relevant facts.

For example, two groups can agree on the basic principle, "Don't harm others *without good reason*," but disagree about whether having committed murder is a good reason for the most extreme kind of harm—capital punishment—because they disagree on the factual question of whether capital punishment deters murder. Many advocates of capital punishment support it because they believe it deters murder and take this to be a good reason for doing the ultimate harm to murderers; opponents of capital punishment often deny that it deters murder and, accordingly, deny that capital punishment can be justified. Assume for the moment that the "maximizing potential" interpretation of equal educational opportunity is as uncontroversial as the principle, "Don't harm others *without good reason.*" Given this assumption, the question of whether Amy was being afforded an equal educational opportunity would be settled by determining whether providing her with an interpreter would, in fact, help her maximize her potential. In other words, the ethical question would turn on an empirical one, in much the same way that for many individuals whether capital punishment is ethically justified turns on whether it deters crime.

In addition to its role in interpreting ethical principles that are generally agreed to, factual information is often a consideration in what ethical principles to endorse in the first place, before they must be interpreted relative to particular actions and policies. This observation is captured by the German philosopher Immanuel Kant's famous dictum that "ought implies can." What this dictum means is that an ethical demand cannot be placed on individuals or groups if the facts make them unable to comply. For example, it is unreasonable to demand of a nonswimmer that he or she dive into the water to save a drowning person.

One especially important and pervasive fact that bounds educational policy is scarcity of educational resources, and any proposals about how to distribute resources must take this fact into account. As an illustration of how scarcity must be taken into account in devising a principle of equal educational opportunity, consider the "maximizing potential" interpretation used by the Rowleys's attorneys. Critics of this interpretation, such as the philosopher Amy Gutmann (1987), contend that if the maximizing potential interpretation were taken literally, then it would surely break the bank. For in order to literally maximize Amy Rowley's potential, much more would have to be done than providing her with an interpreter—she would also need the best teachers, individual tutoring, more time in school, and on and on. To take a more extreme example, how many resources would have to be expended before a severely brain-damaged child's potential was maximized? Finally, insofar as maximizing potential is a principle of *equal* educational opportunity, what would it cost to maximize the potential of *all* children?

These criticisms of the maximizing potential interpretation of equal educational opportunity may have satisfactory answers. We raise them not to refute this particular interpretation, however, much less to suggest that Amy should not have been provided with an interpreter. Instead, we merely intend to illustrate the general point that evaluating an ethical principle requires taking into account how it is bounded by, or fits with, relevant factual constraints.

In addition to the observations that ethical principles are bounded by the facts and must be interpreted in terms of them, there is another way in which facts and values intermingle: Concepts often have both *descriptive* and *evaluative* meanings (e.g., Howe, 1985). Take the concept of intelligence. An IQ score is a quantitative description of a certain portion of an individual's mental abilities relative to other individuals. In this way, an IQ score is "objective," "scientific," and so forth. On the other hand, an IQ score is also evaluative of an individual's mental capabilities—being intelligent is generally considered a good thing to be. Indeed, if IQ failed to be associated with capabilities that society values, if it were merely "what IQ tests measure," then it would be useless and uninteresting (in much the same way that counting the hairs on students' heads would have no use in evaluating and formulating educational policies). The same general point applies to the concepts of achievement, attitudes, critical thinking, and the like—high achievement, positive attitudes, and skill in critical thinking are all considered to be good things. In terms of the Rowley example, insofar as the Court declared that Amy was receiving a "benefit," and insofar as the grounds for this claim were in turn based on Amy's achievement and positive attitudes, the notions that achievement and positive attitudes are goods ("benefits") found their way into the Supreme Court's decision.

In general, some notion of what is good to accomplish will underlie *any* deliberation about the goals—achievement, social adjustment, or whatever—that education should promote, and therefore will have ethical implications. Although one may (and sometimes should) dispute the implicit value judgments embodied in various concepts, as well as their implications for educational policy, denying that such judgments exist only serves to disguise them as wholly factual and "objective." Ignoring implicit value judgments increases the chances that judgments of someone's worth—"So and so will never be a contributing member of society"—will sneak in under the guise of an "objective" evaluation of his or her capacities—"So and so's IQ is 75." Although both of these descriptions might be used to justify the same policy, only the first provides a clear picture of what is being claimed, ethically speaking.

Facts and values, then, intermingle in at least three ways. First, where ethical principles are settled, the facts are required in order to determine whether a given ethical principle is satisfied. Second, where ethical principles are unsettled, it is necessary to establish some reasonably clear link between the facts and the ethical principle in question. Ethical principles are circumscribed by facts, by the dictum that "ought implies can." Finally, a host of concepts have both descriptive and evaluative uses. As we intimated above, this last feature is of particular importance in special education. Given their role, special educators have to be especially alert to the implicit value judgments that attend categorizing individuals as handicapped, LD, MR, EMR, EBD, and so forth, in order to help eliminate the real dangers associated with "labeling." The general point is that none of these concepts *merely* describes a "fact" about someone.

What factual information is crucial to the *Rowley* case? If the facts are uncertain, how might the uncertainty be reduced? In what ways would deciding the facts in one way rather than another affect the position you would hold?

MORAL PHILOSOPHY

The law and the relevant facts establish some very rough boundaries for ethical deliberation. Although by their very nature these boundaries must remain rough, they can nonetheless be substantially sharpened by appeal to a field of inquiry that historically has been devoted to this task, namely, moral philosophy.

The basic aim of moral philosophy is to develop theories that explicate and systematize standards of ethical deliberation that may be used to evaluate ethical choices. Broadly speaking, there are two kinds of ethical theories: principle-based and virtue-based. As a first approximation, these two kinds of theories may be distinguished in the following way: Principle-based theories typically first identify some principle and then apply it to determine the morally right choice in a given situation; virtue-based theories typically first identify the characteristics of the ethically virtuous person and then determine the morally right choice in a given situation by asking how the ethically virtuous person would deliberate in that situation.

In what follows we will further flesh out the differences between principle- and virtue-based theories, as well as differences between two kinds of principle-based and two kinds of virtue-based theories. Our aim is to provide a general characterization of four theories of ethical deliberation that have been influential in the Western philosophical tradition. We will endeavor to treat each kind of view as evenhandedly as possible, but, for the sake of making our discussion manageable, will have to gloss over much of the great subtlety and sophistication that fully developed versions of these theories possess. For the bulk of this section we will continue to speak in relatively general terms, using the example of Amy Rowley for purposes of illustration. Once the necessary groundwork has been laid, we will focus on special education specifically.

Principle-Based Ethical Theories

There are two basic types of principle-based ethical theories: consequentialism and non-consequentialism. We will describe and evaluate each in terms of the *Rowley* case.

CONSEQUENTIALISM. Consequentialism is the view that the rightness or wrongness of a given action should be judged in terms of its consequences. Its most common form is utilitarianism, and we will use the terms *consequentialism* and *utilitarianism* interchangeably.

Utilitarianism holds that one principle will suffice for the whole of ethics: *Actions or policies are right when they maximize the total good.* For example, if the question is whether to devote more tax dollars to education of the gifted or to education of those with handicapping conditions, the choice will be whichever policy produces the greatest good. In this way, utilitarianism promises a calculus of sorts that will always provide an answer to the question of what the right thing to do is. Furthermore, utilitarianism claims to be fair insofar as each individual's good counts equally in the calculations to be performed. Classical nineteenth-century utilitarians like John Stuart Mill advanced utilitarian deliberation as a rational means of responding to increasingly complex industrialized societies; they saw utilitarianism as progressive, as a way of fulfilling the values of liberty and equality by ensuring that all citizens were included in deliberations about the right policy choices.

The intuitive idea behind utilitarianism is by no means strange. It fits perfectly well with a large majority of common ethical beliefs. Rules in schools against cheating, stealing, disturbing others, destroying books, and so on, can easily be justified in terms of the belief that such prohibitions maximize the good. Indeed, only in rare cases will utilitarian reasoning and our common ethical beliefs clash. If this were not true, if utilitarian thinking did not respond to something very pervasive in ethical deliberation, it would never have captured the imaginations of formidable moral philosophers.

Its initial plausibility notwithstanding, when efforts are put forth to develop utilitarianism as a comprehensive "stand alone" ethical theory, several difficulties arise. One difficulty is what to use as the "good" to be maximized. Is it happiness? pleasure? preferences? income? These proposals have historically been offered by utilitarians, and each has been criticized either because, like happiness, it is too vague and variable among individuals, or because, like income, it captures only part of what goes into the truly good life. A second difficulty concerns the frequent inability to actually perform the calculations that utilitarianism requires. Even setting aside the problem of how to define the good, it is highly unlikely that anyone could really determine whether a policy that, say, devoted a larger proportion of resources to the education of those with handicapping conditions or one that devoted a larger proportion to the education of the gifted would lead to the greatest good. A third difficulty is whether *acts* or *rules* should be the object of utilitarian calculations. In the case of Amy Rowley, for instance, should the question be what particular action in this particular case would lead to the greatest good, or should it be what rule would lead to the greatest good in the long run, insisting that the rule be followed even if following it does not maximize the good in the particular circumstances? Finally, utilitarianism encounters problems regarding what is typically called "distributive justice." Distributive justice is one of those issues, no doubt the most important one, where critics charge that utilitarianism yields conclusions that conflict with common moral beliefs.

To illustrate the problem, consider the case of Amy Rowley with respect to the question of how utilitarianism would distribute educational resources. Ignoring once again the difficulties associated with actually trying to calculate what would maximize the good, suppose providing Amy (or the group of children like Amy) with an interpreter would not maximize the good. In that event, utilitarian reasoning would dictate that Amy should not be provided with an interpreter. To extend the example, suppose that even the initial services provided to Amy—the hearing aid and instruction in sign language—would not maximize the good either. To extend the example still further, suppose that the result of P.L. 94-142 in general has been to compromise maximizing the good. Suppose in each case that educational resources would yield a greater "good" (where the "good" is measured by the nation's Gross National Product, for instance) if they were devoted to science education for the talented rather than to education of those with handicapping conditions. Given these suppositions, utilitarian reasoning would dictate the same choice in each case: Resources should be diverted away from those with handicapping conditions and toward those talented in science.

To many, the above kinds of policy conclusions appear to be clearly calloused and unjust, and, incidentally, are ones that most utilitarians themselves would neither be comfortable with nor happily endorse. A utilitarian might well respond that the suppositions about the facts needed to generate the seemingly unjust policy, namely, that people would be most happy with a policy that denied educational opportunity to those with handicapping conditions, are false. The utilitarian could then go on to conclude that utilitarian reasoning leads to unjust policies only "theoretically," not in the real world. A utilitarian might also respond by augmenting the principle of maximizing the good with some "threshold principle." In the case of education, this would mean that the principle of maximizing the good can come into play only after everyone, including those with handicapping conditions, is provided with an education up to some threshold (or "decent minimum").

There are other responses that a utilitarian might make, which we shall not pursue. As we indicated earlier, we are unable to consider ethical theories in all their subtlety and sophistication. We turn now to non-consequentialism, and will use utilitarianism as the point of departure for our discussion.

NON-CONSEQUENTIALISM. According to non-consequentialists, there is no way out of the difficulty with distributive justice for utilitarians. For non-consequentialists, the problems with utilitarianism are not merely theoretical. Furthermore, they charge that using things like threshold principles to augment the principle of maximizing the good is illegitimate within a utilitarian framework because such principles cannot themselves be justified in terms of maximizing the good.

Non-consequentialists focus on the fact that utilitarianism (at least if it is to be consistent) restricts itself to maximizing the good as the only ethical consideration. As a result, principles of justice, as well as other common moral rules, and rights and duties, have force only so long as they are consistent with maximizing the good. To take the example of rights, children like Amy Rowley would have no *right* to special educational services (nor indeed to any educational services at all) except insofar as granting such a right would contribute to maximizing the good. Likewise, children like Amy Rowley could not make claims on the basis of justice unless such claims were consistent with maximizing the good. But rights and justice, or so non-consequentialists would argue, are not the sort of things that should be held hostage to whether they maximize the good. Consider, for instance, the right to free speech in those cases where it leads to turmoil, such as in the civil rights marches led by Martin Luther King Jr. A utilitarian would have to say that if these activities decreased the overall good—happiness, pleasure, or whatever—then King's right to free speech could have (should have) been denied.

Viewed in another way, the problem with utilitarian thinking is that although it requires Amy Rowley to be *treated equally*—her good counts the same as anyone else's in utilitarian calculations—it does not thereby require her to be *treated with equal respect*—her special situation and needs as a person conceivably may be ignored. Again, this is not a conclusion that utilitarians would happily endorse. However, non-consequentialists contend that it is unavoidable so long as utility is the only ethical consideration deemed legitimate.

Non-consequentialists insist that the principle of utility is *subordinate* to other ethical principles (see Benjamin & Curtis, 1986); that is, other principles, especially justice, must check or "trump" the application of the principle of utility. Although non-consequentialists grant that it is often legitimate to maximize the good, maximizing the good should not be the primary consideration if it entails "using" individuals as "mere means" to the welfare of others. That is, individuals should not be required to sacrifice their good solely in order that others may benefit more. For example, an individual should not be deceived into participating in medical experimentation, even if the research holds great promise to advance medical treatment and thereby benefit a large number of other patients. Similarly, children like Amy Rowley must be granted equal respect as persons; their needs must be considered and insofar as possible met, even if this entails decreasing the overall quantity of good that others might enjoy. In this way, justice "trumps" the principle of utility.

Non-consequentialists claim other advantages for their view in comparison to utilitarianism. First, because it is not based on calculating the greatest good, it does not require that some common measure of the "good" be defined that applies across persons. Second, because it is based on principles that apply independent of consequences, for example, "equal respect for persons," it does not require that the consequences of ethical and policy choices be known before a decision can be reached.

Like utilitarianism, non-consequentialism captures basic and pervasive intuitions about ethical deliberation; also like utilitarianism, it encounters difficulties when it is advanced as a complete, all-encompassing ethical theory. One problem that plagues non-consequentialist theories is what to do when different ethical principles conflict. For example, the principle of equal respect for persons could be used to justify allocating a disproportionate share of educational services to those most in need. However, this might conflict with another principle, that of merit, which could be used to justify allocating a disproportionate share of educational resources to the most talented, on the grounds that they had in some sense earned them and would be most likely to appreciate and make good use of them. Indeed, it might be argued that allocating educational resources on the basis of merit itself fits the principle of equal respect for persons. In general, because non-consequentialism provides no method by which to rank conflicting principles, choosing one principle over the other seems to rely merely on intuitions and gut reactions. Utilitarianism, by contrast, provides a way of resolving such conflicts of principles (at least theoretically): It dictates choosing the principle that maximizes the good.

A related problem with non-consequentialism (and one that it shares with utilitarianism) is that principles may be difficult to apply, even when they are not in conflict with one another. Consider the principle of equal educational opportunity. This principle is non-consequentialist when it is interpreted to apply independent of the consequences with respect to maximizing the good. Although it might provide guidance regarding how to evaluate the general ethical viewpoint embodied in P.L. 94–142, namely, that special educational needs ought to be respected, it provides very little guidance when it comes to specific cases like Amy Rowley's. For example, how far should a policy go in providing Amy with special resources in order to ensure that her educational opportunity is equal? And at what point are the children who would otherwise receive the resources being spent on Amy being denied equal respect in order to achieve equality for children like Amy?

On this note we will temporarily leave the discussion of principle-based ethical theories; we will further refine our characterization of them subsequently in the process of developing our characterization of virtue-based theories.

In what ways do utilitarian and non-consequentialist ethical theories illuminate how to decide the *Rowley* case? Which one of these theories do you believe is in general more satisfactory?

Virtue-Based Ethical Theories

At the beginning of this section we distinguished between principle-based and virtue-based ethical theories by indicating that the former use basic ethical principles as the criterion for judging the rightness of actions and policies, whereas the latter use a model of the virtuous deliberator. We will begin our discussion of virtue-based theories by expanding our initial characterization of what distinguishes them from principle-based theories.

Principle-based theories (1) identify ethical principles, (2) evaluate ethical choices in terms of how well they fit with those principles, and (3) are abstract. Virtue-based theories (1) identify the ethically virtuous person, (2) evaluate ethical choices in terms of how well they exemplify the deliberations of the ethically virtuous person, and (3) are particularistic. So far we have had little to say about the way in which principle-based theories are abstract. A discussion of their abstract nature will help clarify an important motivation for virtue-based theories.

One of the ways in which principle-based theories are abstract is that the principles embraced must satisfy *universality*, that is, they must be applicable to all "relevantly similar" cases. Because principles are by their very nature "open-textured," this variety of abstractness gives rise to the problem of how to apply principles to concrete cases. In the *Rowley* case, for example, "equal educational opportunity" posed just such a problem of application regarding whether "maximizing potential" should be the criterion for allocating services and, if so, just what that meant and how far it should go. According to virtue-based theorists, this kind of abstractness encourages ignoring the peculiarities of given situations by forcing them to fit this or that ethical principle and to be "relevantly similar" when they are often unique. In this way, principle-based theories, or so virtue-based theorists would argue, are legalistic, backward looking, and blind to the kind of creativity required when new situations must be confronted for which the principles derived from past deliberations are inadequate.

A second way in which principle-based theories are abstract is that they presuppose *impartiality*. That is, individuals must apply the principles indifferently so that in making ethical choices, personal histories and family and community relationships are pushed into the background or altogether ignored. According to virtue-based theorists, this severely distorts ethical deliberation, because individuals, when they are confronted with ethical choices, can (and should) neither forget who they are and where they come from, nor ignore the special attachments and obligations they have to family and community. For example, it would be somewhat odd, and by no means obviously praiseworthy, for Amy Rowley's parents to dispassionately agree with and endorse the Supreme Court's decision regarding their daughter, even if they believed that this is the view that a truly impartial person would take. Yet, this is precisely what principle-based ethical theories would seem to demand.

Virtue-based theories do employ basic ethical principles—rules against lying, cheating, stealing, and so forth—but virtue-based theories are quick to abandon principles when they appear inadequate for the concrete situation at hand, and to rely instead on a model of ethically virtuous deliberation. For example, suppose the question was whether Amy Rowley's parents did the right thing by taking their case to court.

The way to answer this question would not be confined to looking for some principle. Instead, looking for an applicable principle would be quickly abandoned in favor of asking whether this is the sort of thing a good (virtuous) parent would do given the particular circumstances. Part of the answer to this latter question would depend on Amy's parents' motives and accompanying emotions, not *merely* on the general validity of the ethical principles employed. Good (virtuous) parents would presumably pursue the case out of love for Amy and in order to benefit her, not, for instance, out of animosity toward the local school board or in order to get their names in the newspaper. They would also be sensitive to the particular nuances of the situation.

At the most general level, virtue-based theories provide an alternative to principle-based theories by replacing the criterion of principles with the criterion of the model of the ethically virtuous deliberator, the deliberator who exhibits what Aristotle referred to as "practical wisdom."

Aristotle held that there is an important difference between ethical and scientific reasoning: Scientific reasoning requires bringing particulars under universal rules, whereas ethical ("practical") reasoning requires being able to size up often new and unrepeatable concrete situations and to respond to them as such. Because ethically problematic situations are concrete and unique, ethical principles often are of little avail. The only way to judge an ethical choice, then, is on the basis of how "skillfully" it was made, in much the same way that one would judge the performance of a physician treating a unique patient or a sculptor working on a unique piece of wood. Aristotle believed that members of a community would be able to recognize (at least upon reflection) the ethically virtuous deliberator, the person possessing "practical wisdom," just as they would be able to recognize the good physician and good sculptor, even though what makes the activity of ethical deliberation skillful or virtuous cannot be captured in a set of explicit principles. Such a deliberator could then serve as the model for evaluating ethical choices.

One important feature of the Aristotelian approach is that it anchors models of the ethically virtuous deliberator in the values held in common by a community rather then in abstract universal principles. This feature is emphasized in current "communitarian" ethical theories, developed by contemporary philosophers such as Alisdair MacIntyre (1981), which maintain that the shared values of a community, rather than abstract ethical principles, are the foundation of ethical deliberation.

A second important feature of the Aristotelian approach is its stress on friendship, love, and family. This feature is emphasized in the "relationist" theory of the contemporary philosopher Nel Noddings (1984), who suggests that the model for ethical deliberation ought to be the caring person (which is roughly the perspective employed above to evaluate the rightness of Amy Rowley's parents' decision to take their case to court). Noddings finds it impossible, if not also undesirable, for human beings to permit abstract ethical principles to override the welfare of individuals with whom a caring relationship has been established. To illustrate Noddings' point in terms of the Rowley example, imagine how Amy's parents would be judged if their approach to their daughter's special needs was to calculate what would maximize the overall good, dispassionately counting all individuals' good, including Amy's, equally. In general, Noddings holds that individuals' moral obligations to those who are close to them—especially friends and family—outweigh concern for the abstract, faceless individuals that may be associated with principle-based theories.

So far, we used principle-based theories as a foil in our characterization of virtue-based theories. As the reader might expect, principle-based theorists have their criticisms of virtue-based theories as well. We shall consider two such criticisms, one serious—that virtue-based theories are "illiberal"—and one not so serious—that virtue-based theories are not really theories at all. We will then suggest how ethical deliberation might encompass both principle-based and virtue-based perspectives.

The not so serious criticism—that virtue-theories are not theories at all—results from the way in which virtue-based theories focus on the uniqueness of concrete ethical situations. The criticism is that because they deny that a system of principles from which correct ethical choices may be deduced can be developed, virtue-based theories are far too vague and open-ended to amount to anything more than unsystematic common sense. To this the virtue-based theorist may reply, and we think rightly, that although they are unsystematic in the sense of being *unscientific*, virtue-based theories are not thereby unsystematic in the sense of being *unreflective*. That is, virtue-based theories do not simply capture what one might rashly say about ethics on a Gallup poll, but what one might say only after sustained critical reflection. Indeed, one of the things that such critical reflection reveals is that ethical problems are often particularistic in nature. Insofar as ethical problems have this nature, then, theories that ignore this in favor of the precision and universality associated with science misrepresent the nature of ethics. To again quote Aristotle: "The educated [person] looks for as much precision in each subject as the nature of the subject allows. . . . It is, for example, much the same to allow a mathematician to argue persuasively as to demand rigorous proof from an orator" (in Bambrough, 1963, p. 287).

Turning to the second objection, because virtue-based theories (communitarian varieties at least) are based on shared community values, they may be criticized for being "illiberal" in the sense that they threaten to impose a particular view of the good life on the members of a community who may not accept it. "Illiberal" is used in the sense that Western democracies ("liberal" forms of government) are based on the premise that individuals ought to have the freedom to adopt and the power to pursue their own view of the good life, constrained only by the requirement that their views do not preclude others from enjoying a like freedom and power. Unlike the first objection against virtue-based theories, this one has no very convincing answer.

Where small and cohesive communities are involved, for instance, Amish communities, the threat that a particular view of virtue and the good life might be wrongly imposed on the members of the community is relatively small. Modern industrial societies, however, lack the kind of agreement on the good (virtuous) life that characterizes small, cohesive communities, and are instead marked by a large number of different communities and conceptions of the good life all existing side by side. Because an "official" view of the good life is unacceptable to a society that is both pluralistic and based on liberal principles, such a society cannot be based on any one particular conception of the good life. Thus, a society that is both pluralistic and based on liberal principles cannot be founded exclusively on a virtue-based ethic.

To summarize our discussions of principle- and virtue-based theories, each may be characterized in terms of three elements: a basic criterion, derivative principles, and subordinate principles. As we are using these terms, a basic criterion is the general standard to which a theory appeals, derivative principles are principles that may be derived from the basic criterion, and subordinate principles are considerations that have ethical weight but only so long as they do not conflict with the basic criterion or derivative principles. The theories we have considered are compared in terms of these elements in Figures 2.1 and 2.2

Should whether one is a parent, regular classroom teacher, special education teacher, or administrator affect the position that one supports, as virtue-based theories suggest? If so, contrast the views that these four kinds of individuals might take with regard to the case of Amy Rowley. If not, what is the flaw in virtue-based theories? Finally, what position on the *Rowley* case would you take, all things considered?

"The View from Nowhere" Versus "The View from Here": Conflicting Ethical Perspectives

Our discussion to this point leads to the following general conclusions about the relative advantages of principle- versus virtue-based

Figure 2.1: Basic Structure of Two Principle-Based Ethical Theories

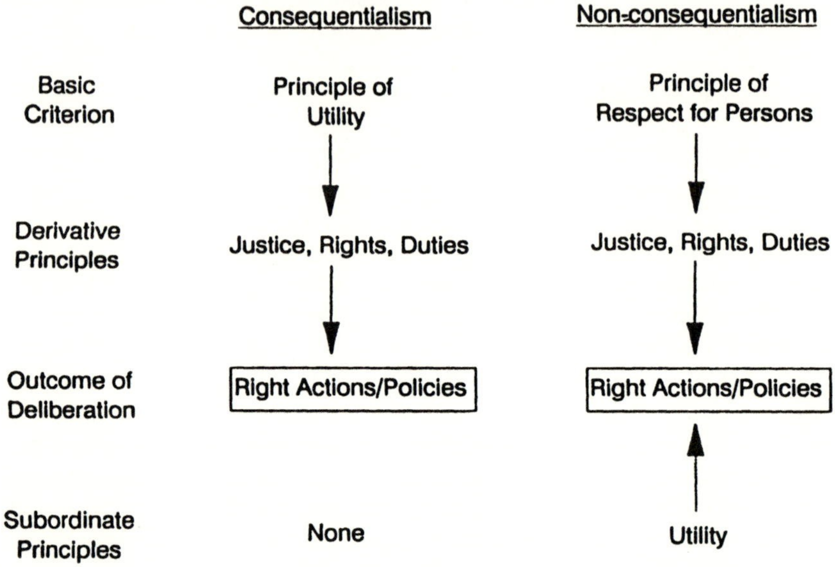

	Consequentialism	Non-consequentialism
Basic Criterion	Principle of Utility ↓	Principle of Respect for Persons ↓
Derivative Principles	Justice, Rights, Duties ↓	Justice, Rights, Duties ↓
Outcome of Deliberation	Right Actions/Policies	Right Actions/Policies ↑
Subordinate Principles	None	Utility

ethical perspectives. The advantage of a principle-based perspective is that because it represents an abstract and universal perspective, it is an *impartial* perspective, one that represents "the view from nowhere" (Nagel, 1986) and that is consistent with liberal principles insofar as it is neutral between particular individual and community conceptions of the good and ethical life. The disadvantage of a principle-based perspective is that it neglects the real and legitimate place for particularity and partiality. The advantage of a virtue-based perspective is that it is sensitive to the particularistic and open-ended feature of ethical choices, insofar as it takes into account the unique features of an individual's personal history, affections, and family and community obligations. In general, a virtue-based perspective is a *partial* perspective, one that represents "the view from here" and gives a special place to a particular view of what will make for a good and ethical life. The disadvantage of a virtue-based perspective is that it becomes "illiberal" if the particular values it embraces are assumed to be binding on everyone.

Our suggestion is that virtue- and principle-based perspectives capture different, but equally legitimate, features of ethical deliberation. Which perspective is appropriate to adopt will depend on the nature of the question to be addressed as well as the way in which the deliberator is situated. For example, it is perfectly appropriate for Amy Rowley's parents to adopt a perspective that is partial to Amy's interests and welfare, and it would be at least odd if they were to adopt an impartial view. On the other hand, it is perfectly appropriate for the Supreme Court to adopt an impartial view, and it would be not only odd, but unethical legal behavior, for them to adopt a view that showed partiality toward Amy. (For instance, a justice who knew the Rowleys personally would be expected to withdraw from the case.)

In general, certain broad ethical principles that apply indifferently to individuals and communities are required for a liberal society to be possible—principles that prohibit discrimination, that provide citizens with equal rights to participate in the political process, that promote equality of educational opportunity, and so forth. These principles are applied universally and impartially to all communities and thereby set boundaries on what individual communities are free to do. P.L. 94-142, for example, requires all communities to provide a "free and appropriate education" to students with handicapping conditions; whether to provide such an education is not something communities are free to decide for themselves. On the other hand, these broad ethical principles leave a certain amount of "maneuver space" in which community and individual values, the concrete and partial perspective, are free to operate. Thus, what constitutes a "free and appropriate education" will depend in no small way on the practices of a given community, particularly the level of educational services it sees fit to provide.

Figure 2.2: Basic Structure of Two Virtue-Based Ethical Theories

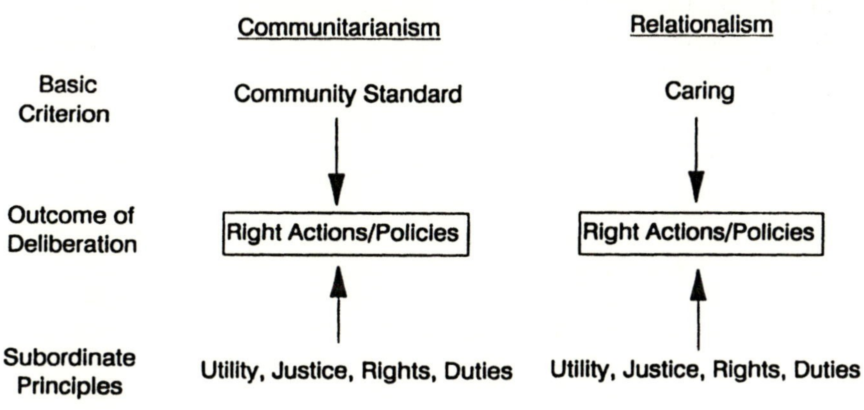

The Perspective of Special Educators: Between the View from Nowhere and the View from Here

Although we believe a kind of peaceful coexistence is possible between the impartial, principle-based and the partial, virtue-based perspectives—between "the view from nowhere" and "the view from here"—we also believe there is no way to wholly or always reconcile these two perspectives when they conflict, that there is no way to completely achieve what the philosopher Stuart Hampshire (1983) calls "moral harmony." This lack of harmony is especially relevant to individuals involved in special education. They must constantly grapple with the problem of trying to balance the general regulations that apply to special education and the values and interests that characterize the individual cases with which they must contend. And instead of being able to assume either one perspective or the other, like the Supreme Court and Amy Rowley's parents are able to do, special educators, because they have attachments both to the general mission of special education and to individual children, must face the difficult predicament of being tugged in both directions.

Unlike parents, special educators must take more seriously the welfare of all students and accordingly must assume a reasonably impartial perspective. On the other hand, there are definite limits to how far this can go, insofar as they have loyalties to their special mission with respect to children with handicaps, to individuals they personally know, and to their particular communities and schools. Special educators thus have "role-related obligations"—in common with other professionals such as physicians, nurses, journalists and lawyers—that are virtue-based insofar as they exemplify what a good professional should be, but also principle-based insofar as they include the requirements of consistency and impartiality. In this way, role-related obligations may be viewed as a sort of compromise, or middle ground, between the view from nowhere and the view from here.

CONCLUSION

In this chapter we provided a broad and general sketch of the various kinds of information and perspectives that are relevant to ethical deliberation—the law, the facts, and moral philosophy—in an attempt to instill an appreciation of its complexity and uncertainty. (To further round this out, readers may wish to consult Appendices B through D. Appendix B contains the code of ethics of the Council for Exceptional Children;

Appendices C and D briefly consider the place of ethical codes and religion, respectively, in ethical deliberation.) We hope to have provided a characterization of the rough boundaries of ethical deliberation that circumscribe the kinds of issues about which reasonable people might disagree and, in the process, to have provided some guidance in the kinds of considerations that go into effective ethical deliberation. We also hope that an appreciation of the sources of complexity and uncertainty associated with ethical deliberation might lead to increased tolerance for the inevitable disagreements that arise and to a commitment to work out common solutions where this is possible and to compromise where it is not.

In Chapters 3 through 5, which deal with more specific issues and cases in the ethics of special education, we will make liberal use of the discussion in this chapter. However, rather than self-consciously and directly "applying" what we have had to say, our method will be to use the discussion in this chapter as a source of concepts and background knowledge on which we may draw as particular issues and cases dictate. We will return to several loose ends from this chapter, particularly the issue of moral compromise, in Chapter 6.

CHAPTER 3

Public Policy and the Mission of Special Education

Our emphasis in this chapter will be on what we have previously referred to as the view from nowhere—the impartial, principle-based view. We will work back and forth between general principles and their application in specific instances, with the aim of further articulating and evaluating such principles. We have selected three general areas for consideration: due process, the distribution of educational resources, and the bureau-therapeutic structure of special education. We will make liberal use of the framework provided in Chapter 2 and will augment it by briefly tracing the history of several pivotal legal decisions and pieces of legislation that culminated in the passage of P.L. 94–142, far and away the single most important influence on special education.

Like so much educational legislation and regulation designed to produce greater equity in the latter half of the twentieth century, P.L. 94–142 has its roots in the *Brown* v. *Board of Education* decision of 1954. Three important principles articulated in this decision are: individuals in modern society need a decent formal education as a condition for a decent quality of life; separating students is harmful to their self-concepts and reduces their achievement; and, following from the first two, separate educational facilities are "inherently unequal" and are therefore prohibited. Of course, the *Brown* decision applied to the issue of separation on the basis of race, not handicapping condition. Nonetheless, much of the basic reasoning has been extended to special education, particularly the appeal to the due process clause of the Fifth Amendment and the due process and "equal protection" clauses of the Fourteenth Amendment.

The first important post-*Brown* decision occurred in 1971. The Pennsylvania Association for Retarded Children (PARC) challenged a Pennsylvania state law that permitted excluding from public school children whom the state certified as uneducable or untrainable. As a result of this challenge, the state agreed to provide access to a free appropriate education for all children with mental retardation, and also to identify all children who had been excluded from public education. Children with mental retardation were also required to be educated in regular classrooms whenever possible.

In 1972, in *Mills* v. *Board of Education*, a more far-ranging set of principles was articulated in a case involving the District of Columbia schools. As in the PARC case, the schools were required to provide a free and appropriate education for all students. The scope of the principles articulated in *Mills*, however, was not confined to children with mental retardation, but included a broad range of mental, physical, and emotional disorders. The principles included individualized educational programs (IEPs) and due process guarantees with respect to placement, suspension, and expulsion. Also, financial considerations were deemed unacceptable for denying education to individuals with handicapping conditions.

The federal government began to take a more active role in protecting the rights of those with handicapping conditions with the passage of the Rehabilitation Act of 1973. Section 504 of this act provides that "[no] otherwise qualified handicapped person . . . shall solely by reason of his handicap, be excluded from participation in, be denied the benefits of, or be subjected to discrimination under any program or activity receiving Federal financial assistance" (quoted in Salomone, 1986, p. 141). In 1974 the act was amended so as to make its application to education unambiguous. The Education of the Handicapped Amendments clarified the definition of individuals with handicaps (who were protected by the act) to include "physically or mentally handicapped children who may be denied admission to federally supported school systems on the basis of their handicap" (quoted in Salomone, 1986, p. 141). The Amendments also required states to submit comprehensive plans for serving all children with handicaps. These plans had to include provisions for due process and descriptions of instructional strategies designed to promote the education of children with handicaps within the "least restrictive environment."

The building momentum in favor of providing an adequate education for all children with handicaps, and the principles articulated in the landmark legal decisions and federal legislation described above, culminated in the Education for All Handicapped Children Act of 1975 (P.L. 94–142). This act made federal financial support for special education services (which, by a sort of "Catch-22," were mandated by section 504 of the Rehabilitation Act) contingent on an effort on the part of the states to identify all children with handicaps, to follow a policy of "zero rejects," and to provide such children with:

1. a free appropriate public education,
2. special education services,
3. related services,
4. the least restrictive environment (presumed to be the regular classroom),
5. due process protections,
6. and individualized educational programs (IEPs).

P.L. 94–142 has encountered some significant resistance, particularly with respect to the issue of cost. Although we count ourselves among those who support the general principles that undergrid P.L. 94–142 and believe it is worth the cost, as our discussions of the issues and cases that form the remainder of this chapter will suggest, P.L. 94–142 is far from a panacea. A solution to one set of problems, it often generates others. Related to this, its implementation is often highly problematic—a pervasive problem that attends any attempt to apply general principles, especially when they are part of a complex bureaucracy.

DUE PROCESS

The principle of "due process" has as its aim ensuring that individuals are deprived of liberties, rights, or benefits only as a result of fair, impartial procedures. (For example, individuals can be sentenced to prison, lose their right to vote, and so forth, only after a "fair trial.") Due process is a non-consequentialist principle, insofar as it applies independent of calculations of how the consequences of a given outcome contribute to maximizing the good. (For example, obnoxious and potentially dangerous political groups like skin heads and Nazis cannot be prevented from publicly expressing their views merely because such expressions might inconvenience motorists, require additional police to be on duty, and so forth.)

The due process protections of P.L. 94–142 are designed to ensure that children are not denied a "free appropriate education"; that they have access to the "least restrictive environment"; and that parents actively participate in and agree to the particular educational goals and instructional methods that are established for their children and formalized in individualized educational programs (IEPs).

The due process protections of P.L. 94–142 (as well as many other provisions) are "legalistic" in two ways: They mandate that schools behave in particular ways by laying down certain procedural rules; and they are coercive insofar as noncompliance can result in the withholding of federal funds. Given the shabby history of U.S. public education vis-à-vis special needs children up to the passage of P.L. 94–142, this kind of legalistic remedy seems warranted (on the model of *Brown*, for instance).

Formalized due process protections for special needs children, however, are by no means free of difficulties. We will consider two cases that depict two pervasive and puzzling problems. First, differences in the knowledge, skills, and attitudes of the various individuals who participate in "staffings" lead to quite different approximations to the ideal of due process. Second, perplexing problems arise at the intersection of due process for special education students and due process for regular education students.

Case: Power Grab in the Staffing

Mary Brown, a fifth grader, was referred for a special education evaluation because she was having difficulties with reading, writing, and organizational skills. Mary was also sometimes disoriented and found it hard to concentrate. Although Mary's mother did not want to have Mary evaluated, Mr. Green, Mary's teacher, enlisted the help of Ms. Jones, the resource specialist, to convince Ms. Brown that the assessment would give Mary's teachers additional information that might aid them in helping her.

Because of Ms. Brown's reluctance about special education, the assessment team agreed that it needed to pay particular attention to performing a complete evaluation. To this end, Ms. Jones administered a larger than normal number of diagnostic tests and observed Mary several times in her regular classroom. Ms. Jones's findings convinced her that although Mary was having several difficulties with her schoolwork, they were not attributable to a handicapping condition that could be verified.

Dr. Anderson, the school psychologist, had been asked to lead the staffing meeting that Ms. Brown attended. The first report presented was from the social worker, who told the group in some detail about the nasty divorce Ms. Brown and her husband were going through, and how it was causing constant tension for Mary at home. Next, Mr. Green presented samples of Mary's work, indicating the difficulties Mary was having completing assignments adequately. Ms. Jones then presented her testing results. She emphasized that she had not been able to verify a learning disability. "Although," she admitted, "my findings are inconclusive, they seem to count against the existence of a learning disability. My classroom observations of Mary indicate that she is under a great deal of stress, and I feel that this best accounts for her current academic difficulties." Ms. Jones gave a couple of examples from her observations, and then said that she recommended modification in the types of tasks Mary was required to perform in class. She indicated that in her opinion such modifications would be sufficient to help Mary cope with her schoolwork until things settled down at home.

Dr. Anderson then presented his report. He began by saying very confidently that his data clearly contradicted the conclusions presented by Ms. Jones. "The WISC–R places Mary in the normal range of responses," he stated, "but the scaled scores for several of the subtests indicate discrepancies in her performance. For example, Mary had particular difficulty with items of temporal-sequential and spatial relationships, indicating impulsivity. Mary's scores also indicate a discrepancy between verbal and performance IQ. Her performance on the maze subtest indicates that Mary has problems with visual perception, organizing objects in space, and planning. Given the overall findings presented, it is clear that the best decision for Mary is that she be placed in special education for a learning disability."

Looking confused, Mary's mother said that although she did not understand much about the tests that were given, it seemed that Ms. Jones and Dr. Anderson did not agree on what was wrong with Mary. She acknowledged that things had been difficult at home and said that Ms. Jones's conclusions about the source of Mary's problems were correct, in her opinion. It seemed to her that if there were such strong differences of opinion it would be better not to label Mary or to put her in special education. "What about Ms. Jones's suggestions for changing Mary's program?" she asked.

Dr. Anderson told Ms. Brown that indeed psychological testing was quite technical and that she really didn't need to understand the complexities of his assessment. "I assure you," he said, "that although diagnosis for learning disabilities is not an exact science, I'm confident that my testing supports Mr. Green's initial conclusion that Mary has a learning disability in reading. Although I'm sure that Suzy [Ms. Jones] made a conscientious effort, I am a certified psychologist and the instruments I administer have proven reliability and validity. As for Suzy's observations, I've never put much stock in that kind of subjective method."

As Ms. Brown tried to reassert herself, Dr. Anderson reiterated his findings and then, turning to Ms. Jones, pointedly asked her if there was a possibility that she had missed something in her assessment. Although very troubled and upset at Mr. Anderson's intimation that she lacked professional expertise, she acknowledged that the possibility of error always exists in any assessment process. Dr. Anderson then remarked that he was sure Ms. Brown would not want to deny her child any of the special benefits available to help her within the school. Checking his watch, he then requested that the staffing move forward since there were only a few minutes left before the next meeting. Thanking Ms. Brown for her attendance, he told her that she need only sign the IEP and Mary would begin receiving special help immediately. Smiling, he passed the papers to Ms. Brown and waited expectantly. She signed, reluctantly.

Should Ms. Brown have signed? Should Ms. Jones have behaved differently? Did this staffing exemplify "due process"?

DISCUSSION. The concept of due process protections within staffings for special education more closely resembles the procedures for informed consent for medical treatment than the procedures for a criminal trial. This is so because the desired goal is collaboration and agreement on the decision to be made, rather than the protection of objectivity and impartiality within an adversarial proceeding, a goal accomplished in criminal law through principles such as the right to face one's accuser, the right to remain silent, and so forth. Given the analogy between special education staffings and the doctrine of informed consent, and the disanalogy between it and criminal law, it follows that parents must be given a reasonable understanding of what is being "diagnosed," by what means, with what degree of certainty, and what the consequences of alternative "treatments" might be. Otherwise their collaboration and agreement are quite perfunctory and hollow.

In the present case, Ms. Brown quite clearly lacked an understanding of the technical language employed by Dr. Anderson—"validity," "reliability," "WISC-R," "temporal-sequential," "maze subtest," and the like. Accordingly, it is difficult to imagine how she could have meaningfully participated in the decision that was made, especially since no one else was disposed to challenge Dr. Anderson. Furthermore, Dr. Anderson's credentials (which he highlighted at one point), the press of time to get on to the next case, the general tenor of the meeting, and her unfamiliarity with the context were each likely to have further intimidated and disempowered Ms. Brown.

For their parts, Mr. Green (the classroom teacher) and particularly Ms. Jones (the resource teacher) could have been more forceful within the meeting, both in expressing their own views and in coming to the aid of Ms. Brown. One would think that because of their expertise and familiarity with staffings they wouldn't be nearly so vulnerable as Ms. Brown. Their failure to challenge Dr. Anderson, or at least to make sure that Ms. Brown understood what was being said, allowed Dr. Anderson to run roughshod over the meeting and reduce due process to a sham.

Dr. Anderson's degree of dominance is perhaps uncommon, but the case of Mary nonetheless serves to illustrate a general (and not uncommon) problem: Formalized due process *procedures* can have their intended effect only if the *processes* employed are faithful to the spirit of due process. For example, consider once again the doctrine of informed consent for medical treatment, and compare Ms. Brown's signing of the IEP with a distraught, confused, and disoriented parent who, overwhelmed by a blizzard of technical medical information, signs a consent form for his or her child to undergo medical treatment.

Several general conclusions may be drawn about due process within staffings from our observations regarding the case of Mary. First, technical information must be presented to parents in terms that they can understand. In our estimation, this is not an impossible task. Parents need not be educational psychologists to understand the gist of what diagnostic testing shows and how learning difficulties may be characterized, any more than patients need a degree in medicine or drivers need a certificate in auto mechanics to understand the "diagnosis" and "treatment." Second, and related to this, it is the responsibility of school personnel not to make unwarranted claims regarding the exactness of their knowledge about the cause and nature of children's learning difficulties and what to do about them. It is also their responsibility not to suppress relevant information, for example, the possible negative effects of labeling. Finally, and related to the first two points, the process of staffings should, as far as possible, approach the ideal of equality among participants. The kind of hierarchical, autocratic process illustrated by the case of Mary obviously should be avoided if due process is to be meaningful. Instead, school people should themselves be treated equally, and, because of parents' especially weak position, a concerted effort should be made on their behalf to ensure that they understand what is being said and are encouraged and empowered to express their views.

Case: Delinquent or Disturbed?

Adams High School was located in the Beecher School District, which bordered a large western city. The Beecher District had a newly elected school board and a newly hired superintendent. Both were committed to a "get tough" policy and agreed to refuse to put up with "criminals" and "delinquents" and to "pander" to them with special programs. Accordingly, the district instituted an unwritten policy that, except in extreme cases and unless strong advocacy existed (typically from parents), violent students would not be referred for emotional disturbances. The policy had resulted in a significantly reduced number of students referred for emotional disturbances and a significantly increased number of expulsions.

John was a tenth grader at Adams and was one of the few students in the Beecher District who had been placed in special education for emotional disturbances. His father, an active member in the ACLU, had threatened to sue when John's former school, Emerson Junior High, attempted to expel John for violent behavior the previous year. At that time he was diagnosed as having emotional disturbances and placed in special education.

John had not been able to cope with a mainstreamed setting at either Emerson or Adams and was therefore in a small, self-contained classroom. Even within this restrictive setting, John was unable to cope. One day, while in what was described by his teacher as an "unprovoked rage," John stabbed another student in the arm with a pencil, broke several windows by throwing large books through them, and hurled a chair at the teacher. He freely admitted these events to the principal and was summarily suspended for 7 days. The principal then referred the matter to the school's student assessment team with the recommendation that John be expelled.

It was 4 days into the suspension before the committee was able to meet to review the case. Because they knew John could not be suspended indefinitely (the legal limit was 10 days), the committee was required to come up with some other solution. As the discussion proceeded, the committee members realized the gravity of the situation. First, an attorney for the district pointed out that unless John's behavior was determined not to be a result of his handicapping condition, he could not be expelled. This, of course, would be extremely difficult, if not impossible, to establish. Second, placing John in a residential setting would be difficult to accomplish quickly because all the available facilities were full. Third, although home tutoring seemed to be the best solution, it was not possible because no one within the school was willing to take on such a burden and there were no available funds to hire an outside person. Thus, the only alternative was for John to return to the self-contained classroom until a more permanent placement could be arranged.

Is the policy that requires schools to serve violent students ethical? Is the unwritten policy regarding referrals for emotional disturbances adopted by the Beecher District ethical? Does it promote due process?

DISCUSSION. Measures taken by school authorities such as suspension and expulsion are punitive in nature. Because they involve various principles that must be observed in order to justify such measures, they come closer to the more familiar model of due process associated with criminal law than the model associated with ensuring informed consent within staffings, discussed in the preceding case (Power Grab in the Staffing), p. 29.

Although regular education students have certain legal due process rights with respect to suspension and expulsion, such rights are more extensive for special education students (though in both cases threats to safety are sufficient to justify a short-term suspension, i.e., 1 to 10 days, without a prior hearing). The extension of more elaborate safeguards for special education students, formalized in P.L. 94–142 and through legal decisions, is largely a response to the historical tendency of schools to exclude troubled and troublesome students whenever they cost schools something in terms of order and efficiency.

Of particular interest in the case of John are three provisions: (1) special education students must "stay put" in their existing placement while (and if) a change in placement is being negotiated and arranged; (2) special education students may not be suspended or expelled if the behavior that constitutes the reason for the suspension or expulsion is a result of their handicapping condition; and (3) educational services may not be withdrawn from special education students (unlike regular education students). Instead, in the event that a particular placement proves unworkable, an alternative, "least restrictive" placement must be found.

These three provisions help explain the decision of the committee in John's case, since it seems to be so clearly guided by and consistent with them. Thus, the committee's decision seems correct, at least from a legal standpoint. But what about the wisdom of the policy to which the committee conformed?

First, the school did not have the needed resources to place John in an environment that would remove the threat of violence to other students and the staff, and a policy that requires such a threat to safety seems clearly objectionable. We have already intimated what the response to this line of argument might be, namely, that schools have a history of excluding troubled and troublesome students. Thus, in order to protect the rights and interests of such students, elaborate safeguards have been devised. Furthermore, to prevent schools from having a too easy way of skirting these safeguards—by claiming a lack of resources—the justification of a lack of resources has been explicitly ruled out. If school districts fail to provide adequate resources, this poses a potential threat to the safety of students and staff. Unfortunately, there doesn't seem to be a better solution. (Though, as we argue in the next section, when the federal government mandates programs requiring additional resources, it could do more to fund them.)

Second, the category "emotional disturbance" often entails exactly the kinds of behavior that are normally the cause for disciplinary action. Thus, if students cannot be disciplined when their behavior is the result of their handicapping condition *and* their handicapping condition is "emotional disturbance," then it would seem that children with emotional disturbances have free rein to do whatever they please without fear of consequences. This kind of criticism may be given a quick response along the lines of our previous observations; however, it also raises some very fundamental and puzzling issues that we will broach several times in this book.

The quick response is that if students with emotional disturbances could be suspended or expelled for the kinds of behavior that they often exhibit—disruptiveness, belligerence, and so forth—then they would be afforded virtually no protection whatsoever. Thus, rather than trying to deal with and help such students, schools could simply exclude them, a practice that was prevalent preceding P.L. 94-142 and that is the clear intent of the "unwritten policy" regarding referrals for emotional disturbances in John's district.

Although we clearly do not endorse this "unwritten policy" (and it is probably illegal given the mandate of P.L. 94-142 to take active steps to locate all children in need of special services), it is useful in ferreting out the deep and puzzling issues we alluded to earlier. In particular, the policy points to the distinctions between moral language coupled with responsibility and therapeutic language coupled with treatment. The first two terms in these pairs refer to the manner in which behavior ought to be described—compare "delinquent" and "disturbed"; the second two refer to what ought to be done about it—compare "disciplinary action" and "behavior modification."

A careful analysis of the nature of and relationships between these opposing ways of viewing human beings is well beyond our purposes here (and would require our venturing into the arena of an ancient philosophical controversy regarding freedom and moral responsibility). Instead, we simply assert that either way of viewing human behavior can be appropriate, depending on the particulars, and that this is reflected in areas such as law and medicine. For example, both law and medicine take moral language and responsibility as the norm and then provide for therapeutic language and treatment by virtue of employing notions such as "not guilty by reason of insanity" and "mental illness" to cover exceptional cases.

Resuming our discussion of John's case, the "unwritten policy" of the district, in effect, seeks to locate as much untoward behavior as possible (possibly all of it) within the way of looking at children associated with moral language and responsibility. In this way, the district would have a moral and, because children would not be protected by provisions of P.L. 94–142, a legal justification for employing punitive measures, particularly suspension and expulsion, for instances of misbehavior.

The district policy is objectionable because it is unwritten and therefore not open to scrutiny; we also believe it goes too far. Though there are obvious dangers in overgeneralizing the therapeutic view to the point where virtually any kind of misbehavior is attributed to a "disorder" or a "disturbance," it is just as obvious that some children truly have emotional disturbances and should be accorded support and treatment. Furthermore, children in general are held less accountable for their actions than adults. That is, our way of dealing with children is in general more "therapeutic" or educational, precisely because they are children who need to be shaped by adults so that they might ultimately take on full adult responsibility.

THE DISTRIBUTION OF EDUCATIONAL RESOURCES

In Chapter 2 we introduced the issue of distributive justice in connection with the discussion of principle-based ethical theories. To briefly recapitulate, questions of distributive justice are questions of how goods (benefits) should be distributed among programs and individuals. As emphasized in *Brown*, among the important goods to be justly distributed in a modern society is education, largely because it serves as the gateway to other goods such as income, employment, and self-respect.

The *Rowley* case is a paradigm of the problem of how educational resources ought to be distributed. Our discussion of the distributive justice aspect of this case served largely to illustrate the application of competing ethical theories, as well as associated criteria for judging the moral acceptability of distributing resources, such as need and expected benefit. In the remainder of this section we will stake out our general position regarding the distribution of educational resources and then discuss three cases.

For K–12 education in general, we endorse what might be termed a "limited equal results" view with respect to the distribution of educational resources (see, for example, Howe, 1989, and Gutmann, 1987). That is, in order for a just distribution of educational resources to exist, each child in K–12 education must, *as far as possible*, attain some "threshold" (Gutmann, 1987) of educational benefit. Such a view is nonconsequentialist insofar as it requires distributing educational resources (at least up to the threshold) on the basis of the criterion of need as opposed to criteria such as merit or talent (which are often associated with utilitarian distributional schemes). Setting aside certain general difficulties with this view (such as how the threshold is to be defined), special education presents peculiar difficulties. For example, for students who are so severely disabled that they cannot reasonably be expected to attain the threshold, interpreting the *as far as possible* condition engenders the difficult problem of determining what an adequate level of support is, short of the threshold. More generally, difficult decisions are required with respect to trade-offs between regular and special education, as well as within special education, which are inevitable given limited educational resources.

Although we endorse a certain kind of non-consequentialist view that makes use of the notion of a threshold, the kinds of distributional questions just described arise regardless of one's theoretical orientation, and, as we have intimated throughout, proposed solutions will often importantly turn on the more concrete factual and legal features of given problematic situations.

Case: Pulling the Educational Plug on Children with Profound Disabilities?

Like so many other school districts in the late 1980s, Grand River District was feeling a severe financial squeeze, which was recently exacerbated by its third millage defeat in two years. A number of cuts had already been made and more were going to be required to balance the budgets in future years. Some of the largest previous savings had come from the special education budget, and it was again being targeted as an area for cuts.

The previous cuts in special education had been achieved largely with regard to mild and moderate needs students, through a decreased reliance on self-contained classrooms in preference to mainstreaming. Now, however, budget cutters were eyeing the severe and profound needs special education program. According to estimates, the cost to the district for the average severe and profound needs student was five times that of the average regular education student, whereas the federal government reimbursed the district only a tiny fraction of the cost (12% of the allocation for a regular education student). The plan was to reduce as far as possible the number of severe and profound needs students served, first by moving borderline cases into regular classrooms and second (and more drastically) by refusing to serve those students judged not able to benefit from what the schools could offer by way of an education.

Shortly after the new policy went into effect, the district refused to admit Tommy Gates, a 5-year-old, on the grounds that because schooling could in no way benefit him, he should not be the district's responsibility.

Tommy's condition was described at a district meeting at which arguments for and against his admission were advanced. He was born 2 months prematurely and, like other such infants, suffered from severe respiratory problems at birth. He later experienced seizures and developed hydrocephalus (water on the brain). Ultimately, Tommy wound up blind, deaf, quadriplegic, and with profound retardation.

In support of the district's position to deny Tommy admission, several pediatricians claimed that parts of his brain had been destroyed (including the cortex, which is associated with cognitive activity) and that he had no potential for learning. Countering the claims of the district, Tommy's parents claimed that he was responsive to sound and to people he knew (for example, he would move his head in the direction of certain sounds and people) and that he exhibited being happy or sad. Tommy's parents denied that he could not benefit from a public education, and they supported their contention with the testimony of a child development specialist who claimed that Tommy could benefit from a program of physical therapy, particularly one that involved frequent handling and positioning of the head. The district remained steadfast in refusing to admit Tommy.

Tommy's parents contested the decision, but additional local agencies, as well as the state department of education, supported the position of the Grand River School District. Eventually, the Gates sued in U.S. District Court. The court ruled that Grand River School District was not obligated to provide educational services to Tommy. The court agreed with the school district that the obligation to provide educational services was contingent on the ability of students to benefit from such services and that Tommy did not have this ability.

Should schools be responsible for children like Tommy? Are children like Tommy capable of benefitting from what schooling has to offer? If so, how? If not, is this a good reason for excluding them from the public schools?

DISCUSSION. Advocates for exceptional needs children are likely to be quite appalled by the behavior of the school district, the state, and the court in this case. Although we disagree with denying Tommy admission to the public schools, in keeping with the spirit of respecting opposing viewpoints and of giving them a fair hearing, it will be instructive to begin our analysis by considering what arguments count in favor of such a posture. As our discussion unfolds, we will move to arguments that count against it.

A fundamental premise of the school district's position is that it cannot supply the services, as an educational agency, that will benefit Tommy. That is, the things that will benefit Tommy, for instance, medical care and physical therapy, are not *education*. Furthermore, this is not simply a result of the way schools are presently structured: Because children like Tommy are not capable of being educated, no amount of additional training, equipment, and so forth, could better enable the schools to perform their function; it simply is not possible. Accordingly, so the argument goes, the school district should not be responsible for providing services that do not fall within its expertise or function. (Compare requiring hospitals to provide an education.)

Not only are the services Tommy requires beyond the purview of public education, but they are also expensive, costing approximately five times what it costs to educate the average child. If the federal government wishes to expand the charge of public education to include serving such children, then it should be willing to *fully* fund this responsibility, rather than funding only a small portion and leaving the rest to local districts, which are often small and underfunded to begin with. At present, such children can receive a public education only at the expense of other children—children in regular education as well as in mild and moderate needs special education.

Such are the arguments that support denying admission to Tommy. How might they be countered? We will begin with what we take to be the weakest counterargument and then consider progressively stronger ones.

One counterargument is to appeal to factual uncertainty about Tommy's ability to respond to educational efforts. (Compare arguments in medical ethics about whether to "pull the plug" on long-term comatose patients.) Although this argument has some plausibility, we believe that it is quite weak. The evidence appears reasonably strong that Tommy is not likely to ever approach the kind of cognitive abilities or "threshold" associated with what is ordinarily expected of school children.

A second counterargument is to expand the meaning of "benefit" to include the sorts of things of which Tommy is capable. This tack avoids the weakness of the appeal to factual uncertainty about Tommy's capabilities. It has the drawback, however, of begging the question against those who would maintain that such benefits are not truly *educational* benefits and therefore are not the responsibility of schools to provide.

A third counterargument is that children other than severe and profound needs students can benefit from inclusion of the latter in schools. An education should include not only mastery of basic academic subjects but also things such as an understanding of the differences between human beings, a tolerance of such differences, and the ability to effectively interact with those who are different. Although this argument is quite powerful when it comes to the practice of integration of mild and moderate needs students, it is considerably weaker when applied to severe needs children such as Tommy, for at least two reasons. First, children like Tommy are typically not integrated into regular classrooms and thus do not have meaningful interactions with other school children. Second, the typical justification for interaction between special and regular education children is that both benefit educationally. To the extent that children like Tommy are not capable of *educational* benefit (a contentious but plausible assumption for purposes of argument), it should give one pause to include such children in public education on the grounds that it will benefit other children. For this makes their right to a public education tenuous (What if other children do not benefit?) and is an affront to their dignity to the extent that it makes them simply a part of the *curriculum* for other children.

Although each raises important issues, the three arguments considered to this point against denying children like Tommy Gates access to the public schools are far from conclusive. There are at least two additional arguments, however, that may be employed to seriously question the actions of the Grand River School District, both of which appeal to broader issues of the distribution of resources vis-à-vis special education than can be accommodated by the narrow focus on *educational benefits* and the traditional functions of public schools.

The first takes the form of a "slippery slope" argument. An argument of this form is one that tries to dismiss certain policies on the grounds that if a certain kind of decision is permitted in a certain case, then the first step has been taken onto a slippery slope and the inevitable result will be a slide to the bottom of the hill. In the present case, to permit the Grand River School District to exclude Tommy Gates is to permit schools to again decide who is "educable" and thus who may attend school, precisely the kind of policy that permitted schools to exclude students with handicaps prior to the PARC and *Mills* cases and P.L. 94–142.

Although we would have to admit that there seem to be some clear distinctions between children like Tommy Gates and mild and moderate needs students (pointing out the possibility of making distinctions is a general kind of response to arguments that take the form of a slippery slope), we have little confidence in school districts to make the best decisions regarding such distinctions, especially when they are under severe financial pressures. The history of public education's treatment of special needs students supports our skepticism. We would add, however, that school districts have a good argument regarding the issue of costs. When the federal government mandates expensive programs, it should be willing to adequately fund them. Otherwise its authority and seriousness of purpose are undermined, and it is asking for significant resistance.

The second counterargument to denying admission to children like Tommy that we believe is strong trades on the current nature of the social welfare system. Like any other parents, Tommy's presumably want their child provided with appropriate services at the expense of the government while they work or pursue other activities. Insofar as institutions other than schools that provide free services do not exist (which is true in Tommy's state), parents have nowhere else to turn. Given such a system of distribution, the nitpicking about whether Tommy is educable or capable of benefitting *educationally* from schooling is beside the point, and the "zero reject" requirement of P.L. 94–142 provides a way for parents to obtain the services they need to lead their lives in a reasonably normal fashion, free of sometimes heavy financial burdens. In our estimation, were alternative, nonschool services readily and freely available for children like Tommy, whether to admit him to the Grand River School District would be a tougher call. Under the conditions that existed, however, he should have been admitted.

In conclusion, we have used the case of Tommy Gates to raise several important issues and arguments. Not to leave the reader with the impression that school districts are free to adopt the policy of the Grand River District, however, we should make clear that they are not. The Tommy Gates case is fictitious but is based on the actual case of *Timothy W.* v. *Rochester, New Hampshire, School District* (see Fischer, Schimmel, & Kelly, 1991, for a brief discussion). Timothy W., whose condition was very much like Tommy's, was denied admission to a school district in New Hampshire. What happened next follows the story of Tommy Gates, including a decision by a federal district court that Timothy could be denied admission on the grounds that he could not benefit educationally. Not included in the story of Tommy, however, is that the decision in Timothy's case was later reversed by the U.S. Court of Appeals. Among the arguments advanced in the reversal were that the zero reject clause of P.L. 94–142 applies with particular force to students with severe handicaps and, speaking directly to an issue we have discussed in some detail, that P.L. 94–142 nowhere requires that special education students be capable of benefitting to qualify for its protections.

Case: Whose Benefits are to be Sacrificed?

At Coolidge Elementary School, in District 6, Sam Bert came to his third-grade classroom looking angry and sullen. He immediately overturned a desk and slammed a chair against it. Betty Cheng, the classroom teacher, managed to get him to a desk in the back of the room, isolated from the rest of the children. As the other children settled into their work, Sam alternated between shouting and uttering incoherent sentences to himself. This went on for over half an hour.

Betty Cheng had come to expect this kind of behavior from Sam ever since he had been mainstreamed into her class at the beginning of the school year. Although she tried to praise Sam whenever he behaved in appropriate ways, she typically found herself spending more time taking away Sam's recess and otherwise punishing him for his outbursts. She also had found it necessary to instruct the other children to ignore Sam unless he behaved appropriately. On his occasional "good" days, Sam was a bright, enthusiastic student who could be academically successful. However, in Ms. Cheng's estimation, Sam in general compromised other children's opportunities to learn, both by disrupting the classroom and by taking up so much of her time.

Sam's special education teacher suggested trying a behavior modification plan, which met with little success. In fact, Sam seemed to delight in accumulating as few points as possible. (Ms. Cheng got the impression that he would have preferred to collect negative points.) Wanting to understand some of the underlying causes for Sam's behavior, Ms. Cheng contacted Sam's mother. Ms. Bert was very frank and told Ms. Cheng that Sam's father had abandoned them and that she was unemployed and experiencing severe financial difficulties. According to Ms. Bert, Sam's father had abused Sam emotionally. She admitted, however, that Sam still loved his father very much. Ms. Bert also said that Sam had recently been a "terror at home and in the apartment complex" and that she had no idea how to control him. She concluded by saying that she felt Sam was the school's problem during the day.

Having exhausted all the options she could think of, Ms. Cheng requested that Sam's IEP be re-evaluated with the aim of having him removed from her classroom. It was 30 days before Sam's case was considered, during which period his behavior did not change. The staffing team recommended a full evaluation for emotional disturbance and gave the assessment team 60 days to complete their assessment, after which time they would again meet.

During this 60-day period, Sam was as unmanageable and as disruptive as ever, perhaps more so. Ms. Cheng could tell by his face (often filled with rage and fear) what kind of day she was in for. He was frequently loud and was generally abusive to anyone within shouting distance. Ms. Cheng's other students did the best they could to ignore him. The only time Sam did any schoolwork was when an adult guided his every step. He was also disruptive and belligerent during lunch and on the playground after lunch.

Ms. Cheng breathed a sigh of relief when, after his re-evaluation was completed, Sam was removed from her classroom and placed back in a self-contained classroom for students with emotional disturbances.

Was this a just decision for Sam? For the other students?

DISCUSSION. Insofar as economic conditions and the level of support provided to social programs external to public education have an important impact on the responsibilities of public education and what it can reasonably be expected to accomplish, this case is similar to the Tommy Gates case just discussed. That is, Sam's home life and his mother's financial condition have an obvious and profound effect on Sam. On the other hand, and unlike the Tommy Gates case, the trade-off of benefits between Sam and the regular education students is relatively immediate and direct, because of Sam's disruptiveness within the confines of the classroom. In addition to consuming what may be viewed as a disproportionate share of resources, particularly teacher time, Sam also actively obstructs other children's opportunities to learn.

Following the reasoning of *Brown* and the findings of educational research, Michael Walzer (1983) has observed that school children are "one another's resources." This observation counts in favor of combining children in classrooms in such a way as to maximize both academic and social benefits—particularly with respect to raising those students most in need up to a "threshold"—and, accordingly, counts against segregating children on the basis of talent and social skills. This line of reasoning entails a presumption in favor of keeping Sam in the regular classroom.

The actions that Betty took were consistent with this presumption (though not necessarily for the same reasons given above), and it would seem that Betty did the best she could given the resource constraints to which she had to respond. Regarding the more general question of educational resources, however, a greater allocation could go a long way toward alleviating the problem she faced with Sam. For example, more resources would permit things such as smaller class sizes, more training for classroom teachers in dealing with troubled students, more resource teachers and aides to work within regular classrooms, and other measures that would help students like Sam directly and that would prevent them from being so obstructive to other students.

On the other hand, the general problem raised by cases like Sam's cannot be altogether eliminated. Even if a dramatic increase in funding for education were forthcoming that would permit students like Sam to remain in regular classrooms (and presumably to benefit), there would still exist the problem of the benefits of some children having to be traded off against the benefits of others. At the very least, teachers would be trading the benefits of some for those of others in terms of how they allocated their time and effort.

Theoretically, a disproportionate allocation of resources can be justified on the grounds that it is fair when based on needs and getting all children up to the threshold. However, in some cases no amount of time and effort on the part of schools may succeed. Furthermore, allocation decisions have to be made under real-world conditions in which, because of resource limitations, it may be impossible to respond to the needs of certain students without sacrificing the needs of others.

The latter situation is the kind of dilemma involved in the case of Sam, and in terms of our discussion of principle-based ethical theories in Chapter 2, the case illustrates the conflict between utilitarian and non-consequentialist principles. Apparently, in the interests of maximizing benefit, Betty and the staffing team elected to place Sam in a self-contained classroom for students with emotional disturbances. The resources available (not available)—both in the school and in the social welfare system—played a large role in producing the problem, and, under these conditions, where resource limitations entail that *someone's* interests have to be sacrificed, it appears there is no escape from endorsing a utilitarian brand of reasoning. This conclusion may be too hasty, however. First, contrary to what we've been assuming so far in the discussion, it could be that Sam himself would benefit more (or at least as much) from an alternative placement. This would remove the uncomfortable conclusion that Sam's benefit must be sacrificed for the benefit of others. Second, even if it turns out that an alternative placement for Sam would not benefit him, one needn't necessarily justify such a placement on the basis of a crude utilitarian trade-off. Instead, it may be viewed as an (admittedly unfortunate) clash between competing *legitimate interests*, namely, Sam's versus the other students', that must be adjudicated in some fair way. When conscientiously and rigorously carried out, due process performs precisely this function of ensuring fairness, and it does so without reference to utilitarian trade-offs.

Case: Must the Gifted Earn Their Placement?

Peter is a ninth-grade student in an urban metropolitan junior high school who has been enrolled in the Talented and Gifted (TAG) program since sixth grade. He had always been a good student who showed an eagerness to learn and had a history of being well liked by his peers and teachers.

In eighth grade, Peter's peer group changed. He began to hang around with kids who wore heavy metal T-shirts, jean jackets, and long hair. Drug talk was frequent among them and actual drug use was a real possibility. Peter talked freely of drug use and the parties he attended. As a consequence, many teachers became concerned and Peter's mother was called in for a conference. Ms. Beck, Peter's mother, confirmed Peter's drug use, but saw it as no more than teenage experimentation and rebellion.

Meanwhile, Peter's grades were slipping, and he was often absent and showed little interest in his classwork. Additional conversations with Ms. Beck resulted in improved attendance, but Peter's behavior did not improve. Although he attended classes, he rarely participated. He was receiving failing grades in the majority of his classes, primarily because of his unwillingness to turn in work.

District funding and resources for the TAG program were limited, and consequently more students were eligible for the program than could be served. This prompted the question of whether Peter should be permitted to remain in the program. Mr. Johnson, the TAG coordinator, believed that the TAG program would challenge Peter and engage him in learning, with the result that his peer group would fade in importance. However, a variety of opinions were expressed by Peter's teachers that were quite at odds with Mr. Johnson's. Some believed that if Peter didn't care they shouldn't either. Others believed that Peter was taking up space in a specialized program that he did not appreciate and from which he seemingly gained nothing. A third group believed that given Peter's intelligence, he should know better and should not be receiving additional services unless he decided to straighten out and take advantage of his gifts.

Since Peter is not responding to the help he is receiving, should he be removed so that a more productive student can take advantage of the TAG classes?

DISCUSSION. Technically speaking, TAG programs are not within the purview of special education because they do not fall within the scope of P.L. 94–142. On the other hand, TAG students fall under the general rubric of "exceptionality," and 45 states explicitly recognize their special status in state educational laws, mandate special programs for them, or both. The existence of TAG programs thus raises important questions regarding the just distribution of educational resources.

As the exchanges about where to place Peter suggest, qualifying criteria for TAG programs, in the minds of some at least, are rooted in the general criterion of merit rather than need. Given this interpretation, special education programs and TAG programs are based on quite different principles. In the case of special education, students qualify because they have special needs that it is the responsibility of schools to try to meet; the question of being excluded because they fail to meet performance criteria—and thus fail to *deserve* or *earn* their placement—does not arise.

When qualifying criteria for TAG programs are identified with merit, such programs become difficult to distinguish from the general practice of talent tracking and are subject to the same kinds of criticisms. For instance, when education is in general underfunded and when a large number of students are not succeeding even minimally, it appears quite unjust to allocate extra resources—in the form of accomplished teachers, small class sizes, superior equipment and curriculum materials, and so forth—for programs for students who are most likely to succeed without such extras. Instead, resources should be allocated in precisely the opposite way—toward those students most in need—to help ensure that as many as possible attain a threshold of educational benefit. Given this tack, it would seem to follow that TAG programs should be dismantled in the interests of a just distribution of educational resources.

Setting aside the argument based on rewarding merit, TAG programs also can be defended on utilitarian grounds. That is, TAG students may be viewed as a particularly valuable resource, or "human capital," that should be developed to the utmost for the benefit of society as a whole. This kind of argument would seem to have a good deal of popular appeal insofar as it fits with the current preoccupation with economic competitiveness reflected in reports such as *A Nation at Risk* (National Commission on Excellence in Education, 1983). As the reader may have already surmised, we are not sympathetic to this kind of argument. First, we are skeptical about whether those who will contribute most to the general welfare can be reliably identified ahead of time and about whether TAG programs can reliably develop such a talent to contribute (see, for example, Bull, 1985). Second, and more generally, because we endorse the kind of non-consequentialist view briefly described earlier, we believe the first responsibility of public education is to ensure that as many children as possible attain a threshold of educational benefit. This does not mean that we dismiss utilitarian considerations altogether, but instead view them (in terms of the discussion of Chapter 2) as "subordinate" to the demands of justice.

To complicate matters, however, not all individuals would rest their justification for TAG programs on criteria such as merit or utility. Instead, TAG programs can be justified on the basis of serving a particular kind of "special needs" or "at risk" population of students, namely, a population that requires different approaches to "benefit" from educational experiences and is therefore in danger of suffering a number of ill effects from schooling, including dropping out.

In our estimation, this defense of TAG programs is more convincing than ones based on merit or utility. However, when viewed in terms of the larger picture, it is a defense of the need for TAG programs only insofar as it is also an indictment of public education in general. That is, TAG programs are needed only because regular education is structured in a way that alienates a large number of students (not just TAG students). Were public schools structured in a way that emphasized inclusion and cooperation more, and sorting and competition less, then TAG programs would be largely unnecessary (as would much of special education).

THE BUREAU-THERAPEUTIC STRUCTURE OF SPECIAL EDUCATION

Whenever the federal government, through the courts or through legislation, mandates that principles must be observed across local jurisdictions, it is inevitable that problems in implementation will arise—because of outright resistance (consider *Brown* and the remedy of busing), unavoidable ambiguities (consider the open texture of terms such as "free appropriate public education"), and the need to articulate specific qualifying criteria for federal funds (consider "needs testing" for certain kinds of educational aid). P.L. 94–142 exhibits all three of these problems. Having already announced our allegiance to its general spirit, we will now focus on the second two.

We have dubbed the structure of special education "bureau-therapeutic." This description is motivated by the manner in which P.L. 94–142 is formulated and operates. In particular, it enumerates eight handicapping conditions: hearing impairments, speech impairments, visual impairments, physical impairments, learning disabilities, mental retardation, emotional disturbances, and chronic or long-term health problems. These categories are "bureaucratic" because they are tied to federal reimbursement for special education services; they are "therapeutic" because they (particularly learning disabilities, mental retardation, and emotional disturbances) require a "diagnosis" (typically arrived at through psychological testing) and an associated "therapy" (as described in IEPs).

The bureau-therapeutic structure of special education engenders a number of difficulties, several of which we will examine in the first two cases considered in this section. In the third and final case, we will consider whether there might be ways to improve special education's general structure—and mission.

Case: "Get My Son Out of Special Education!"

Jason Giles attended Willoughby elementary, a school in a large urban district with a high concentration of black and immigrant Latino students. Jason himself was black and 8 years old. He had been placed in a self-contained classroom for the mentally retarded 2 years previously on the basis of teacher recommendations, low achievement, and IQ testing. Although he was doing quite well vis-à-vis his IEP, his resource teacher determined that his end-of-year evaluations indicated his placement should remain the same, that is, he should remain in the self-contained classroom for children with mental retardation.

Jason was the youngest of four siblings living with his mother, Melissa Giles. The family had been getting by on state assistance ever since Jason's father left, 9 years previously. Ms. Giles had never involved herself much in her children's schooling. She was deeply skeptical about the American dream of upward mobility for people like her and her children, and felt powerless and ignorant when it came to her children's education.

All this was about to change. After years of despondency and just barely getting by, Ms. Giles had decided to take control of her life and the lives of her children. She was now working part-time, pursuing a college degree in accounting, and had become active in civic groups such as the NAACP. She also developed a keen interest in her children's education and how the schools were responding to them. For example, whereas she had previously viewed Jason's placement in special education as a matter for the schools to decide, she now viewed it as a consequence of the harmful and perhaps even racist structure of schools with respect to minorities. For although Jason was subdued and helpless in school, at home he was quite curious and loved to ask questions, especially about how things worked.

Ms. Giles vowed to challenge the school. When Jason's end-of-year evaluation meeting was held, Ms. Giles arrived with a folder under her arm and fire in her eyes. As the meeting began, she immediately took the floor and declared that she wanted Jason out of special education. Opening her folder and glancing at its contents, she asserted that IQ tests are racially biased and that they set up a self-fulfilling prophecy for black children. "Labeling so many black children mentally retarded is an atrocity that severely limits the possibilities of success for black children within the schools," she said. She went on to say that she had been doing some research and had found that blacks and other minorities make up a disproportionate share of children placed in special education in the district, and hinted that a lawsuit might be in order.

Taken aback, the principal, Ms. Fairchild, said that she regretted that Ms. Giles saw things the way she did. "Our aim at Willoughby," she said, "is to help all our children reach their full potential. The fact that Jason is black has nothing to do with how we treat him. It is his needs and abilities that we respond to." At this point the school psychologist, Ms. Hampton, joined the discussion. She pointed out that the school district had made a concerted effort to locate culture-fair tests and that, in any event, IQ tests were highly predictive of student performance and were only one factor used in deciding how to place students. Achievement and teacher recommendations were others (though she conceded that minority representation on school staffs and on assessment teams was rare). She continued that it was an unfortunate fact that some children were developmentally slow and that Jason would "drown" if placed in a regular classroom. Trying to sound more encouraging, however, she said that if Jason improved substantially, he eventually could be placed in a regular classroom.

Ms. Giles was obviously prepared for what she heard. Responding to the principal, she pointed out that the expectations that schools have toward groups of children can have important consequences for what schools take their potential to be, and that the expectations for blacks were typically low. Responding to the school psychologist, she expressed skepticism about there being any such thing as a culture-fair test, and about other factors weighing very heavily in placement decisions (particularly given the lack of school staff versed in cultural and linguistic issues), and that IQ tests were highly predictive only because they predicted success in a white world. In addition, she asserted that it is quite unlikely for children to work their way out of special education, given the stigmatizing effects of labeling and the watered-down curriculum that only puts them further and further behind.

These exchanges continued for about 40 minutes, at which point Ms. Fairchild said it was time to end so that the next staffing could begin. She told Ms. Giles that if she was still firm in her position, another meeting would have to be arranged to resolve the conflict. Ms. Giles (looking defiant but pleased) said she had not changed her position one bit, and agreed to a subsequent meeting.

How would you evaluate Willoughby's placement practices in the case of Jason Giles? What should Willoughby do?

DISCUSSION. One of the peculiar features of this case is that rather than pressing *for* special services, Ms. Giles is pressing *against* them. Of course, unlike students who prompted *Mills*, PARC, and P.L. 94-142, students like Jason Giles aren't excluded from public education per se but, through a kind of ironic twist, are excluded from regular education because of the existence of special education.

The bureau-therapeutic nature of special education looms large here. Consistent with this notion, various scholars in special education have observed that it often operates on the model of medicine. That is, an ailment (disability) is identified, laboratory (psychological) tests are devised for detecting it, and therapies (IEPs) are prescribed. Although overly simplistic even in medicine, this model is generally serviceable there. A serious difficulty that plagues such a model in special education, however, particularly regarding things such as mental retardation, is the manner in which it locates disabilities (for example, on the model of tumors) *within* individuals in a way that abstracts them from social context and cultural background. Furthermore, the model assumes that there is some objective way to determine when the disability is present.

It would clearly be absurd to blindly presuppose this model and then to administer an IQ test written in English to Spanish-speaking children to determine whether they have mental retardation or learning disabilities. (But it's been done! See, for example, *Diana* v. *Board of Education* (1970); Miramontes, 1987.) Short of such glaring examples, giving standardized IQ tests to children like Jason Giles is subject to the same kind of difficulties. Among other things, a flag is raised whenever, as in the case of the Willoughby district, a disproportionately high number of minority children are placed in special education; for such disproportions are prima facie evidence that some systematic and discriminatory bias is operating in placement decisions. This is precisely the point of departure that a U.S. District Court took in *Larry P.* v. *Riles* (1979). The court went on to argue that the "equal protection clause" of the Fourteenth Amendment requires a burden to be placed on schools to demonstrate that placement criteria (IQ testing was the particular focus) that result in a disproportionate number of minorities (Larry P. was black) being placed in programs for the mentally retarded bear some "rational relationship" to the goals of education. Invoking a strong presumption against racial discrimination, the court declared that IQ testing could not meet this burden.

In the *Larry P.* case, the school district admitted that its tests were probably not culture-fair; it claimed instead to be using the best ones available. Without venturing into the controversies about the nature of IQ and the possibility of devising culture-fair tests (which we believe would be a dubious and misguided undertaking), it would seem wise to significantly downplay or preferably to eliminate IQ testing (the practice in

New York) in educational placement decisions. One of the objections to such a policy, of course, is that it results in less "objective" and "scientific" evidence to appeal to in making placement decisions, forcing such decisions to rely more heavily on school people's judgments and thus actually exacerbating the problems of bias. Insofar as information on IQ is only *apparently* objective and scientific (recall the discussion in Chapter 2 of the value-laden nature of educational concepts), forgoing it only serves to make more clear how tenuous and uncertain decisions about educational placements are. In light of our earlier discussions of due process and informed consent, this would be a good thing for all concerned.

P.L. 94–142 is not silent on the issue of cultural bias in placements. Indeed, it explicitly prohibits placing children in special education when the sources of poor school performance are the result of cultural or linguistic differences with existing school norms. In an attempt to prevent discrimination against them, however, minority students may unadvisedly be denied special education services due to ignorance about such cultural and linguistic differences and about appropriate instructional strategies for such students. (We will examine a similar issue in the case called, Special Education: Opportunity or Stigma?, p. 70.) These conflicts arise, in our estimation, from the general propensity of schools (a propensity by no means confined to special education) to identify and sort children to make them fit into the system as it exists, rather than permitting the myriad backgrounds and needs that children bring to schools to dictate the forms that curricula and teaching should take (Miramontes, 1990; Miramontes & Commins, 1991).

Our discussion of the Jason Giles case has focused largely on *how* to place children in the categories enumerated in P.L. 94–142, and we have suggested in particular that placement should not be so heavily influenced by IQ testing. But there is a broader and, indeed, prior question, which we hinted at in the immediately preceding paragraph, of *whether* children ought to be placed in such categories at all. There is growing sympathy for answering "no" to this question and moving to "noncategorical" schemes. We will consider the advantages and disadvantages of such a proposal in our discussion of the next case.

Case: Reverse Incentives

Laurel elementary was a progressive school in which special education and regular education had developed a close working relationship. Laurel's approach was not only in line with, but ahead of, recent changes in state policy. At the end of the previous school year, the state guidelines for special education were changed to a noncategorical approach that resulted in a dramatic increase in the number of special education students who were to be integrated into the regular classroom. This change in state policy was felt to be long overdue by the principal and staff at Laurel, who were wholeheartedly in favor of the new emphasis on integration. Indeed, Laurel had already made plans to integrate the majority of special education students it served when school started in September. As part of the plan, special education teachers were to be integrated into team teaching situations with the regular classroom teachers.

The integration plan was implemented as planned at the start of the school year. Regular teachers received immediate feedback and consultation from special education teachers regarding students they perceived to be having difficulties. As a result of the close collaboration between the regular and special education teachers, the need for referrals and staffings for special education services declined and accordingly far fewer students were staffed into special education classes.

Ironically, Laurel's success at integration had a cost. At the end of the school year, Mr. Brown, Laurel's principal, received word from the district that Laurel would be losing one of its special education resource teachers the following school year because of the declining enrollment in special education. In the district's eyes, there was a declining need and justification for special education resources at Laurel.

What should Mr. Brown and Laurel's staff do?

DISCUSSION. One of the important things the case of Laurel elementary illustrates is that noncategorical schemes do not really eliminate the need to categorize. Instead, in an effort to reduce the stigma attached to labeling, to redirect the emphasis on identifying children's handicaps to addressing their specific needs, and to foster integration—all laudable aims—such schemes simply reduce the number of categories of special education students. Given the current state of policy, categorization cannot be eliminated altogether because of qualifying criteria for federal funding for special education articulated in P.L. 94–142. As a consequence, schools have a "reverse incentive"—an incentive not to do these things—when it comes to eliminating categorization and implementing thoroughgoing integration plans.

In response, some scholars (e.g., Stainback & Stainback, 1984) have suggested largely dismantling the special education bureaucracy, particularly with respect to mild and moderate needs students, and replacing the present "dual system" of regular and special education with a single system that would eliminate the problems of labeling and segregating special education students. Other scholars (e.g., Lieberman, 1985; Mesinger, 1985) find this suggestion quite worrisome. In their estimation, although the goals of eliminating the dual system are good ones, they have little confidence that schools would respond in a way that would not be harmful to special needs students. Adopting a somewhat cynical attitude (but one that is supported by history), they fear that special needs students would be denied extra resources and would be simply thrown into regular education and allowed to sink or swim.

Although we, too, agree with the aims of eliminating the dual system, we also agree that such a policy shift has significant dangers, especially if viewed in isolation from the larger policy context. Of particular importance is the mixed funding scheme—local, state, and federal—for public education. Historically, in the interest of promoting equity, the federal government has seen fit to create educational programs to supplement local and state educational resources where educational programs are expensive, have weak local constituencies, or both. The catch is that federal aid is inevitably accompanied by the requirement that special education students meet qualifying criteria in order to ensure that money is really needed and that it will be used for the specific purposes for which it is intended. Thus, as long as schools remain dependent on federal aid for special education resources by virtue of the present mixed funding scheme, some type of qualifying criteria, or categorical scheme, would seem to have to remain in place. Accordingly, schools like Laurel will face some version of the "reverse incentive" problem in their attempts to thoroughly integrate special needs children.

One proposal to alleviate this problem would be to separate the processes of referral and staffing from what goes on in the (integrated) classroom. Given such a strategy, identifying a student as fitting this or that special education category would be used only for the purposes of justifying claims for special education resources. Labels would not be used in the local schools, and resource teachers would collaborate with regular classroom teachers on the model of Laurel.

This strategy would seem to be largely consistent with existing policies and, for this reason, it may be the best solution that is available. On the other hand, it has at least three drawbacks. First, conducting business as usual with respect to referrals and staffing is likely to reinforce the very kinds of attitudes and practices associated with distinguishing the "turf" occupied by special versus regular education that schools like Laurel seek to change. Accordingly, it increases the likelihood that special education students will need to have their special problems "diagnosed" and then will need to be "treated" by special educators. Second, even if this problem is avoided, it seems a major waste of time and effort to continue with this kind of "paper compliance," which renders referrals and staffings sham procedures designed only to satisfy bureaucratic demands. (As an illustration of this problem, Shepard, 1987, found that in Colorado the cost of identifying students as learning disabled consumed all the resources made available by P.L. 94-142 to provide special education services for them.) Finally, there is no guarantee that schools in general would adopt the same commitment to integration exemplified at Laurel. Instead, they might simply garner special education resources and then, under the guise of a noncategorical/integrative approach, place their special education students in regular classrooms and provide them with little or no special help.

To make real headway, it appears a more radical change is needed than the half measure of separating the processes of referrals and staffings from the other, more specifically educational practices in schools. In particular, the current method of financing education needs to be overhauled in such a way that resources would be distributed toward those children and schools most in need, independent of the precise causes and categories associated with such needs. That is, the dual system of curriculum and financing should be dismantled (at least with respect to mild and moderate needs students) in favor of a more thoroughgoing needs-based system. For why should it matter, for instance, whether a child is merely a "slow learner" or is learning disabled? In each case the aim should be to provide the child with an adequate education.

This strategy, too, has several drawbacks. First, it requires some scheme of school finance that would be quite different from the one that is currently in place, both *among* and *within* schools. This, in turn, would likely require federal funds to be disbursed in a quite different manner. Without providing much by way of detail (we provided a more detailed discussion of the distribution of educational resources in an earlier section of this chapter), in both cases resources should be distributed on the basis of need so as to ensure that as many children as possible obtain an adequate education. Second, such a thoroughgoing needs-based scheme of finance would also require major changes in the attitudes and practices that pervade much of public education, particularly with respect to distribution *within* schools. Were schools to persist in sorting and tracking children according to their perceived talents in the face of a funding scheme that didn't earmark resources according to categories of need, then students most in need would likely be the losers (precisely the objection raised by those who oppose abolishing the "dual" system). Finally, such a dismantling of the current structure of special education would threaten special educators, both personally and professionally. This is an issue that we will take up in the next case.

Case: Pull-out is Best

Over the past year there was a move in the Twin Mountains School District special education program to institute a greater degree of collaboration with regular education. In particular, the resource teachers had been asked to minimize pull-out programs in favor of integration. The motto adopted by the district director of special education, a motto that was endorsed by many of the special education staff, was: "Our mission is to work ourselves out of a job."

Betty Rheems, a resource teacher at Oak elementary, wholeheartedly supported the direction in which the district was moving, and she was anxious to get started on the collaboration efforts in her school. Janet Peterson, the other resource teacher at Oak, held a different view. Ms. Peterson had long aspired to be a special education teacher. After spending her first several years of teaching in the regular classroom, she decided to go back to the university to major in special education. Just 2 years previously she completed the requirements for certification and became a resource room teacher. Although Ms. Peterson endorsed the ideal of integration, she was skeptical of integration in practice. On the basis of her personal experience, first as a regular classroom teacher and then as a resource teacher, she believed that the needs of special education children were rarely met in an integrated setting. She valued her specialized training and believed it had equipped her to work with exceptional students much more effectively than her regular teacher certification program had.

Although she acknowledged that much of the research on pull-out programs indicates that they are stigmatizing, she believed that, on balance, special needs children benefit from the specialized instructional strategies that originally attracted her to special education. Stigma, she thought, was largely a "social" and "attitudinal" problem, not intrinsic to special education, and she believed that regular classroom teachers could do much to counteract it if they would only make the effort. In her opinion, more, not fewer, special education services were needed, and fewer is what she perceived to be the implication of the new district policy. Also, she resented the implication that what she did was not "special" and that her job could be done by any regular classroom teacher with only a modicum of advice and additional training. Ms. Peterson was thus quite reluctant to participate in the intensive efforts required to make the integration of the special education students into regular classes successful, and was quite uncooperative with both Ms. Rheems and the regular classroom teachers.

How would you respond to Janet?

DISCUSSION. Convinced that only she and others like her care enough and have the required skills to "save" the "huddled masses" of special needs children from the cold and harsh reality of public education, Ms. Peterson may be one of those special educators who suffer from the so-called "Statue of Liberty" syndrome. On the other hand, her concerns may not be so easy to write off. As we observed in several of our previous discussions, advocates for exceptional students are quite justified in counseling extreme caution with respect to proposals to dismantle special education. For, in the absence of major changes throughout the entire public education system, such proposals pose a genuine threat to the interests of special needs children. Again, the lessons of history should not be forgotten.

Setting these concerns aside and adopting a more optimistic attitude regarding the present and future responses of public education toward special education students, what new mission and roles might special educators adopt for themselves? Should they really become committed to working themselves out of a job?

Giving a simple "yes" to this last question would be more than a little Pollyannish. A rather large special education constituency presently exists—complete with federal, state, and local bureaucracies; certification programs in universities; parental pressure groups; special education teachers themselves; and a community of special education researchers. The vested interests that these groups have must in some way be accommodated; they are highly unlikely to passively sit by and watch much of special education go by the boards. And the question is not merely one of raw self-interest. Many individuals, like Ms. Peterson, are deeply and sincerely committed to special education and, in addition to having devoted time, effort, and expense to it, have their personal values and identities bound up with it. For this reason, too, they are unlikely to passively permit special education to be dismantled. Finally, there are indeed important things that special education has to offer, and, even though we believe it should be structured differently, it ought to remain in place in some form.

Special education for severe and profound needs children (which we have largely bracketed for the purposes of the present discussion) might be preserved largely in its present form. Special education for mild and perhaps moderate needs children, however, ought to gradually wither away. Over time, it should be replaced by a needs-based system that responds to all children. Such a system would eschew sorting and talent tracking, and would equip and require regular education teachers to work with students of all kinds. Resource teachers could serve as consultants and advisors regarding how to respond to special needs students, a role that might very well be required permanently.

How feasible is this proposal? Again, it is crucial to avoid being Pollyannish. In addition to resistance to restructuring from within special education, resistance is also likely to come from without, as a consequence of the current drive for "excellence" in education. The drive for excellence encourages using merit and talent for the purposes of sorting and tracking, criteria and practices that threaten special needs students. The associated goals of accountability and of raising test scores encourage "turfing" students into special education so as to exclude low scores from the data that will be used to evaluate the performance of schools and their personnel. This provides an illustration of how current educational policy trends are at cross-purposes—namely, the trend toward integration versus the trend toward excellence—and is a good lesson in the dangers of attempting to view the mission and structure of special education apart from the broader political and policy arena.

CHAPTER 4

Institutional Demands and Constraints

In this chapter we move down one notch in abstractness and up one notch in the power of special educators to immediately affect the welfare of students. The issues and cases in this chapter best represent what we previously characterized as "between the view from nowhere and the view from here."

Although P.L. 94–142 provides general guidelines regarding what services must be provided for special needs children, the law has, as we observed in the preceding chapters, an "open texture" and is otherwise limited in the ethical guidance it can provide. As a consequence, what actions to take and policies to formulate in particular contexts ultimately falls on states, school districts, schools, and individual teachers. Given their peculiar "role-related obligations," special education teachers are increasingly called upon to negotiate and broker services for students with special needs, especially as more and more of these students are integrated into regular education classrooms. These negotiations have a significant ethical dimension and often require special education teachers to take stands that put them in conflict with school and district administrators, other special education teachers, and regular classroom teachers. At times, they are also faced with "stretching" or "finessing" P.L. 94–142 itself for ethical reasons.

INSTITUTIONAL UNRESPONSIVENESS

Both schools and district special education programs may be counted as "institutions," and one of the most frustrating features of such institutions for special education teachers is the often slow and cumbersome way in which they respond to the demands of particular situations, especially new ones. A further difficulty is that special education teachers are often expected to be loyal to institutions themselves and, accordingly, to accommodate the demands of particular situations to the overall good of the institution. The implicitly utilitarian nature of institutions, combined with their slowness to respond, often puts special education teachers in conflict with various school officials. Special education teachers must represent the interests of the particular special education students with whom they have a personal relationship within the context of the particular demands of the daily routine, not solely from the more removed and abstract interests that make up the "greatest good" for institutions in the long run.

Case: Broken Promises

Laura Rosen is 31 and has 6 years of experience teaching in a special education resource room. Toward the end of the school year she was asked by the district director of special education to consider transferring the following year to another school in order to open a new primary class for severe needs students (the school in question had never before provided such services). Ms. Rosen had little prior experience with severe needs students (some of whom need help in activities such as feeding themselves and personal hygiene, for example), but she was ready to try something new and welcomed the challenge. Ms. Rosen was somewhat concerned, however, about having sufficient materials and supplies for the class, since an appropriately supplied classroom did not exist at the school to which she would be moving. She agreed to the transfer after she met with the director of special education and received assurances that adequate funds were available and that she would receive what she needed in time to begin the new class.

During the summer Ms. Rosen filled out purchase orders that would have expended about half the money she was allotted. She intended to wait until after she got to know the students and could be more specific about their particular needs before deciding how to spend the rest of the allotment. In September, as she began to set up the classroom, she discovered that most of the orders she had written had been delayed and were just being sent out. In order to have the necessary materials to begin the school year, she found herself having to borrow what she could from the primary teachers in her building. Although the principal was sympathetic, she claimed that no funds were available to meet Ms. Rosen's immediate need.

By November Ms. Rosen was extremely concerned. Not only was she still waiting for many of the materials ordered, but she was told by her special education supervisor that the funds she had earlier held in reserve were no longer available. In addition, the materials she had borrowed at the beginning of the year had to be returned, and she was thus left with a woefully undersupplied classroom. A discussion with the principal yielded results similar to those of September.

When several of the parents began to comment on the lack of materials available to their children, Ms. Rosen decided to enlist their help. (In general, Ms. Rosen thinks parent volunteers are important in her program, and many of the students' parents participated in tutoring and other classroom activities.) Because of their active participation, many of the parents had been aware for several months of the limited resources. They had, in fact, often supplied games and books from their homes to supplement Ms. Rosen's meager supply. Consequently, they were eager to help. They wrote a letter in support of Ms. Rosen's request for more materials and took it upon themselves to talk to the principal about the matter. The principal continued to voice support, but again insisted that she was unable to allocate additional funds for this program and suggested that they call the special education office directly.

The following week Ms. Rosen received a visit from the special education director. She was reprimanded for what was characterized as "unprofessional" behavior—involving the parents in a matter that, according to the director, should have been handled internally. She was also informed that a letter to this effect would be placed in her personnel file.

What should Ms. Rosen do?

DISCUSSION. Because of the fast pace of activities within school districts, priorities are constantly shifting. As one fire is put out, another tends to flare up and the one that preceded it is quickly forgotten. In this case, one fire was put out when a new class was created to meet the needs of a certain group of students and an experienced teacher, Ms. Rosen, was recruited to teach it. A new fire started when the materials Ms. Rosen had ordered failed to arrive and funds she had been promised were withdrawn. Her attempts to go through normal channels were to no avail. As a consequence, she found herself facing the dilemma of either demonstrating her loyalty and "professionalism" by getting along without the basic materials she had been promised, or going outside normal channels to apply pressure and work around institutional roadblocks in order to meet the needs of her students. She seemed to have no alternative but to enlist the support of parents.

From the perspective of the special education director, however, Ms. Rosen's actions were perceived as challenging the lines of authority, that is, as "unprofessional," and presumably as having the potential to damage the reputations of both the school and the district's special education programs in the eyes of the community. Perhaps the situation would have turned out differently, and Ms. Rosen could have avoided the reprimand, if she had persisted a bit longer in her efforts to obtain the funds that the special education director had promised. On the other hand, the director reneged on her initial promise and was unresponsive to Ms. Rosen's later appeals, and it was now 2 months into the school year. From Ms. Rosen's perspective at least, it would seem that either the original agreement was made in bad faith or once Ms. Rosen agreed to teach the class (and this fire was put out), the director no longer perceived any need to be responsive.

Lurking below the surface of Ms. Rosen's dilemma are fundamental questions about the degree to which special education teachers ought to be respected as professionals who contribute importantly to decision making and whose views ought to be afforded careful attention. Also raised are questions about the degree to which parents should be involved. In this case, Ms. Rosen was more or less expected to be a good soldier and to accept, without question, decisions from higher up in the institutional hierarchy. She was also expected to maintain appearances and to keep the parents satisfied.

The issue of teacher professionalism (or lack of it) is a large and complex one that is by no means restricted to special education. But it is complicated for special educators because their role as teacher involves not only the ordinary level of school bureaucracy, but also an additional layer of special education program administration. The lines of authority, therefore, are likely to be more numerous and less clearly drawn than in regular education. The individuals along those lines of institutional authority, especially the special education director, were clearly an important part of the problem in this case. However, the director's behavior was not something Ms. Rosen could do anything about, at least not very quickly. Thus, and we think rightly, she did what she thought best for her students, by refusing to simply be a good soldier.

The issue of parental involvement is a bit more complicated. Although institutions rightly seek to settle their own problems and to avoid airing their "dirty laundry," the role that parents play (or should play) in their children's school is often ambiguous. On the one hand, a major thrust of special education legislation has been to increase the involvement of parents in their children's special education programs. (In fact, enlisting the aid of parents is avowed as a major aim of most regular school programs as well.) On the other hand, Ms. Rosen's dilemma points to the ambivalence of school personnel toward encouraging parents to become fully involved in the workings of schools. Insofar as parents participated as classroom volunteers in Ms. Rosen's program on a daily basis, it is reasonable to assume that they were already becoming concerned about the limited resources provided for their children and were already beginning to voice those concerns. Thus, even if Ms. Rosen *did have* some power to persuade parents not to rock the boat, it is by no means clear that she *should have* exercised it.

In addition to being caught between parents and the special education director, there was another source of difficulty for Ms. Rosen, namely, the school principal. In particular, it would seem reasonable to expect the principal to have taken a more active role in the resolution of this conflict, especially since it was the principal, not Ms. Rosen, who suggested to the parents that they call the district special education office.

At least two factors may have contributed to the principal's reticence: social relationships within the building and the district-wide method of resource allocation for special education. First, because Ms. Rosen was new to the building, she had had little opportunity to develop a strong working relationship with the principal, which potentially put her (and her students) at a disadvantage in comparison to the rest of the teaching staff. Although this might be the *explanation* for the principal's behavior, it is no *justification*. The resources students receive should depend on their needs, not on how effective their teacher is within the social network and how good he or she is at manipulating the system. Indeed, it would seem that a principal should be especially protective of a new teacher.

Second, the situation may have resulted from the way in which resources are distributed to individual schools within the district. If funds for special programs are not included in the school's general operating funds, and are instead allocated through the district special education office, then the principal is provided with little room to maneuver with respect to special education. Such a system of allocation would certainly make the principal's behavior more understandable, if not also more defensible. Nonetheless, it still seems reasonable to expect the principal not to, in effect, abandon Ms. Rosen and her students. Because the principal both failed to help in the negotiations with the special education director and was unwilling to provide any materials from the school's supplies, she seemed to view Ms. Rosen and her students as merely physically present (and perhaps also as a drain on school resources) rather than as genuine participants in the school.

In conclusion, Ms. Rosen's dilemma resulted from both the structures of institutions and the behavior of certain individuals within them. By their very nature, institutions will respond more slowly to particular situations than individuals involved in those situations would like. Furthermore, administrators must unavoidably adopt a relatively abstract perspective that tries to balance numerous competing demands. However, the availability of *basic* student resources should have received immediate attention.

It appears that Ms. Rosen's dilemma was largely avoidable. First, the lines of communication between Ms. Rosen, the principal, and the special education office should have been more open. Second, Ms. Rosen clearly should not have been misled by the special education director into thinking that resources would be available when they would not be, for this amounts to deceiving her into accepting an assignment she might otherwise have refused. Finally, if the principal had simply used her position to provide Ms. Rosen with some needed support, the situation would have had a much better chance of being satisfactorily resolved.

Case: Negotiating the Handicap

Elm Elementary School, located in a mid-sized suburban district, is overcrowded and short of staff. Many of the students it serves have special needs, and a relatively large number of students are in special education. Elm has only one special education resource teacher, Fred Rodriguez, who serves 31 students. District policy dictates a minimum of 32 students in order for a school to have more than one special education teacher.

For the past several months there have been very few referrals to the special education program, largely because Elm instituted a child study team that functions very effectively and handles student problems in a way that keeps students in their regular classrooms without additional services. Part of the reason for the success of the study team, however, is that Elm's teachers have increasingly come to Mr. Rodriguez for advice and other help with their students in order to make the process work effectively.

Although he is very supportive of this process, Mr. Rodriguez is also very frustrated by the heavy work load it entails for him, and he believes he is unable to give his own students the kind of attention they need. His increased interaction with the building teachers also makes it very difficult for him to meet all the demands of his job. When he talked the situation over with the principal, Ms. Thompson, she reminded him that adding only one more child to the special education program would permit him to work with 16 rather than 31 students and would also provide more support for the teachers in meeting the needs of their diverse population—a goal Ms. Thompson very much desires.

As a consequence of this conversation, Mr. Rodriguez found himself trying to find a good candidate for special education services. Eventually Sally, a fifth grader, was referred for an emotional/behavioral disorder (EBD) because of her sullen and disruptive behavior in class, and a full evaluation was conducted. In the staffing meeting, the data presented indicated that Sally had a speech disorder. Although it could not be considered severe, it might have been the cause of Sally's frustration and, in turn, of her recent disruptive behavior. Testing results were inconclusive, and there was no other event that could be identified that would explain her change in behavior.

If it was determined that Sally had an emotional/behavioral disorder, Elm school would get an additional special education teacher; if her behavior was determined to be the result of a speech/language disorder, services would be provided by an itinerant speech language therapist. Sally's parents were very concerned about the stigma attached to an EBD label, but put their trust in the staffing committee and agreed to accept its recommendation. Mr. Rodriguez was in a position to tip the balance of the decision in either direction.

What should Mr. Rodriguez do?

DISCUSSION. Mr. Rodriguez could always challenge the seemingly rigid policy that requires at least 32 special education students in order for the district to provide more than one special education teacher, and then treat Sally's designation as a separate issue. One problem here is that changing policy can be exceedingly slow (as we pointed out in the previous case). Furthermore, the problem captured in the saying "you have to draw the line somewhere" is unavoidable when it comes to questions of distributing limited resources. In any event, our focus in this case is on what the situation demands in light of existing policy constraints.

Given that Sally's designation and the prospect of getting a new special education teacher are intertwined (at least for the near future), Mr. Rodriguez's problem boils down to a host of trade-offs among the welfare of different individuals and groups—his own, Sally's, other students' and teachers' at Elm, and other students' and teachers' in the district.

In light of uncertainty about what will benefit Sally most, the evidence suggests that a designation of emotional/behavioral disorder for Sally is unwarranted, or at least premature. All other things being equal, an EBD designation could be harmful to Sally, since her display of undesirable behavior was, after all, quite recent and might very well be a consequence of her speech difficulties or perhaps of as yet unidentified difficulties. It would be far better to try a wait and see approach, using the itinerant speech/language therapist to work with Sally while monitoring Sally's progress. Furthermore, Sally's parents should be encouraged to take a more active role in exploring her emotional difficulties as part of the wait and see strategy.

Should Sally fail to improve or get worse, then a designation of emotional/behavioral disorder would be more justified. Such a designation would presumably benefit all concerned at Elm by providing the additional special education teacher that would lighten everyone's load and thus provide more attention to both general education and special education students. (The downside is that, in the competition for resources, Elm's welfare might come at the expense of other schools in the district whose needs are just as great or greater.)

So far we have been assuming in our discussion that Sally must be the chief beneficiary of whatever decision is made. However, one might take a much more utilitarian tack that focused more exclusively on the welfare of Elm as a whole. In particular, one might argue that it is not only Sally who has to be considered but all individuals at Elm, and that whether Sally would benefit or not, designating her as having an emotional/behavioral disorder would maximize the good for others at Elm—teachers as well as students. (The kernel of such an argument is implicit in the remarks of the principal—remarks that prompt Mr. Rodriguez to wonder whether he isn't looking for one more special education student merely as a pretext for getting the additional help he thinks is so sorely needed.) Such crude utilitarian reasoning is subject to the sorts of criticisms we advanced in Chapter 2. However, this tack would be much more palatable if Sally could receive dual services—for both her emotional problems and her speech and language problems. Indeed, such a combination of services might also make it possible to resolve her problems more quickly than they otherwise might be.

To summarize our general position, if Sally would benefit more from being designated as having an emotional/behavioral disorder than a speech/language disorder, then the case is strong for doing so, since all concerned (at least at Elm) would benefit. The same reasoning would apply to providing her with dual services. The case would be weakened if other schools in the district had an equal or greater need for additional special education resources. The case would be weakened further if Sally would not benefit or would actually be harmed by being designated as having an emotional/behavioral disorder, such that Sally's welfare was being sacrificed for the welfare of others at Elm.

By way of a concluding observation, it is worth noting that if not so much depended on the decision made in Sally's case—namely, whether Elm would be assigned an additional special education teacher—how to describe her problem would probably not prompt such intense scrutiny and reflection. And yet, cases such as Sally's should serve to motivate one to reflect on the importance that *all* such decisions regarding how to describe children in terms of special education classification have for their welfare.

SPECIAL EDUCATION TEACHER AS BROKER

Special education teachers are trained in the details of the P.L. 94–142, which provides the framework for procedures that guide the determination of both what constitutes a handicapping condition and the range of legally required services. In this respect, special education teachers are more similar to administrators, who are responsible for ensuring compliance with laws within schools, than to regular education teachers, who have only a passing acquaintance with the laws that apply to education. As *de facto* interpreters of the law, special education teachers have an ethical obligation to enforce not only its letter, but its spirit as well. This obligation, in turn, often requires special education teachers to act as advocates for the rights of special needs students.

The consulting role of special educators brings them into daily negotiations with regular education teachers, staff members, and administrators. Using their more intimate understanding of particular special needs students and the nature of their handicapping conditions, special education teachers must often negotiate "deals" to obtain the services they believe should be provided for the special needs students they represent. In order to be able to distinguish a good deal from a bad one, special education teachers must have a firm understanding of the role they play in brokering opportunities for students, as well as a commitment to the spirit of P.L. 94–142.

Case: Resistance to Integration

Jane Rollins is a resource room teacher in a junior high school. Her classroom includes students with learning disabilities as well as students with emotional disturbances. She has recently met with the special education supervisor regarding her efforts to meet the goal of integrating students into regular classrooms. Ms. Rollins had been trying over the course of the first semester to integrate five students and had consistently met with a great deal of resistance from the teachers she approached. By the end of the semester, no teacher had agreed to work with her. One teacher reflected the prevailing attitude of the regular education teachers when she remarked that "problem students" belonged in the resource room, for this improved the "learning environment" in regular classes. This teacher went on to suggest that bringing these problem students into the regular classroom, as Ms. Rollins was advocating, would jeopardize what the regular education teachers would be able to achieve with their students.

Although Ms. Rollins knew that the principal, Mr. Jones, rarely took a stand on any issue, she nonetheless decided to ask him for help. Mr. Jones was sympathetic but reminded Ms. Rollins that he did not believe in "interfering" with the way "his" teachers handled their classes. He also expressed his belief that the success of integrating special needs students ultimately depends on the goodwill of regular education teachers and that "ordering" anyone to comply would only undermine integration efforts. He did, however, offer to talk to Mr. Young, the new social studies teacher.

Mr. Young was not enthusiastic, but seemed to have been intimidated by Mr. Jones. As a new teacher, he had five different class preparations and was still learning his way around. He was not sure how he could accommodate the special education students and also feared that Ms. Rollins would be evaluating his teaching performance. After Mr. Jones assured him that he need do no more than permit Ms. Rollins to meet with her small group in the back of his class, he agreed to this arrangement.

When Ms. Rollins explained integration to Mr. Young he listened politely, but then referred to his conversation with Mr. Jones. He told Ms. Rollins that because the principal approved, he didn't mind if she met with her small group in the back of his room, so long as she took total responsibility for "her" students. Mr. Young also had other conditions. He insisted that he had to maintain high standards in order to encourage students to learn and, to be fair, he could not have a double standard for grading. Thus, he felt Ms. Rollins should also take full responsibility for grading her students. In addition, he suggested that it would be very helpful if she could work with one of his more "difficult" groups of students on a regular basis.

Should Ms. Rollins accept Mr. Young's deal?

DISCUSSION. This case illustrates the difficult role the resource teacher must play in gaining access for special education students to the "least restrictive environment." Ms. Rollins assumed an advocacy role on behalf of her students and is contemplating the "deal" that would permit them to be integrated into the regular classroom. The terms of the deal pose two problems: how far to stretch the meaning of "integration," and the lengths to which she should go to try to personally ensure that the deal will work.

Ms. Rollins is specifically charged with upholding the law with regard to the "least restrictive environment" requirement of P.L. 94-142. However, she can rightly ask herself if she should be the only individual in the school with this responsibility. Indeed, if this responsibility is not generally shared by the members of the school, especially by the principal, Mr. Jones, integration is virtually impossible to achieve. Unfortunately, Mr. Jones does not take this responsibility very seriously: He both failed to take a leadership role and, by his example, encouraged resistance to integration on the part of regular education teachers. Because Ms. Rollins has received virtually no support for the general idea of integration, her problem devolves into one of evaluating the terms of the "deal" with Mr. Young, which offers a significantly watered-down variety of integration (if indeed it qualifies as integration at all). In particular, Ms. Rollins must determine how to best discharge her responsibilities in the situation within which she finds herself—a situation in which the aims of integration have already been drastically compromised.

Mr. Young's offer poses several dangers. For example, if Ms. Rollins agrees to go along with Mr. Young's peculiar kind of "integration," her students may be even more stigmatized than if they were isolated in a separate room. Since Mr. Young identifies integration with permitting special education students to be present in the same classroom with regular education students but otherwise segregating them, the arrangement he proposes could actually accentuate students' awareness of differences by providing a constant reminder of them. A further danger of accepting Mr. Young's offer is that it creates a sort of "Catch-22" for Ms. Rollins. If the arrangement *does not* "work," then resistance to the very idea of integration could be fortified within the school. The catch is that if the arrangement *does* "work" the results could be nearly as bad for Ms. Rollins. It could result in entrenching within the school a highly diluted conception of integration and could lead to increased expectations for her to participate in more of this kind of integration (in classrooms other than Mr. Young's, for instance), including taking special responsibility for "difficult" students.

Despite these dangers, there are several reasons that count in favor of accepting Mr. Young's proposal. Because this is the first opportunity Ms. Rollins has been given to attempt integration in any form, it might be unwise not to try to make the best of it. This could open her up to a charge by Mr. Jones that she was given the chance to try integration but refused. Furthermore, she might be able to "educate" Mr. Young regarding what true integration means and why it should be supported. She might, therefore, be able to negotiate with him for a more acceptable arrangement for her students. Conceivably, making this kind of progress with Mr. Young could be instrumental in changing the attitudes and beliefs of other teachers in the school.

On the other hand, even if he were to change his attitudes, Mr. Young very likely lacks influence within the school, due to what might be called the "new teacher initiation ritual." Because Mr. Young is untenured and new to the social system of the school, he has inherited the tasks (and often the students) that other teachers in the school do not want. Mr. Young was, in effect, pressured into working with Ms. Rollins largely because of his vulnerability as a new teacher. This "initiation" is not uncommon and raises questions concerning the responsibilities of all teachers, in both special and regular education, to create an atmosphere of mutual respect and shared responsibility within the school environment as a whole. The "initiation ritual" obstructs the cultivation of collegiality, mutual respect, and professionalism; it also indicates the existence of a hierarchy of rank and privilege, a pecking order, where "power" comes with seniority and tenure. In Ms. Rollins' school the principal did nothing to try to challenge these norms; indeed, a cynic might quite plausibly suggest that Mr. Jones occupies a comfortable position atop the hierarchy, which he manages to camouflage by ostensibly setting teachers free to run their classes as they see fit.

Ms. Rollins' dilemma ultimately boils down to how much of a risk she is willing to take with both her own interests and the interests of her students, in light of the tremendous uncertainty about the outcomes of taking Mr. Young up on his proposal. Trying to determine what is best, *all things considered*, is no easy task. Indeed, we would give Ms. Rollins different advice. Howe thinks the misunderstandings of integration among the school faculty are so pervasive and the risks of undesirable outcomes associated with cooperating with Mr. Young so great that Ms. Rollins ought to back out of the deal and wait until she can create a more promising opportunity. Miramontes acknowledges the misunderstandings and uncertainties, but thinks the risks are nonetheless worth taking. She is skeptical that things will ever improve otherwise, or at least that they will improve quickly enough.

LABELING

Given the present structure of most special education programs, it is necessary to group students into categories, both to define their particular difficulties and to determine the associated special services they require. These categories, in turn, serve as the basis for allocating educational resources.

An unintended and unfortunate consequence of the need to categorize special education students is the well-known problem of "labeling." Numerous studies in the field of special education have documented the negative effects of labeling. Results of such studies show, for example, that compared with nonlearning disabled students, learning disabled students are generally held in lower esteem by teachers, classmates, and parents. Other labels such as emotionally or behaviorally disturbed (where the perception is that the problems are more serious and perhaps associated with home life, mental illness, moral shortcomings, and so forth) carry an even greater stigma. In addition, studies have also demonstrated that individuals from various minority groups are more prone to be overidentified for special education programs than individuals from the cultural mainstream. Labeling is further complicated by the difficulties of determining whether a student's problems are caused by a handicapping condition as defined by the law. Although noncategorical and integration strategies have promised to alleviate some of the problems associated with labeling, both by helping regular classroom teachers and students and special education students to become more familiar with one another and by reducing the need to apply labels in order to receive services, labeling remains a serious problem that will not go away in the near future.

Case: Special Education: Opportunity or Stigma?

Manuel is a fifth grader. He is a migrant child and has been in and out of Sky Elementary School over the last several years. This year he is having more difficulty than usual keeping up with schoolwork and is lagging far behind in reading. Mr. Fry, his teacher, is very concerned. He has taken Manuel's case to the child study team in his school. He explained that Manuel's problems in reading stem from an inability to understand the content, a short attention span, and a seeming lack of motivation. The study team suggested that Mr. Fry give Manuel some individualized reading instruction, concentrating on building vocabulary. Mr. Fry tried this, but because of Manuel's absences and the need to attend to the 32 other students in his class, he found it difficult to work with Manuel consistently. Manuel was also beginning to exhibit signs of stress in the classroom by acting out and being aggressive toward classmates. Since there were no special reading services available in the building, Mr. Fry eventually returned to the child study team to seek an official referral for special education testing. The team decided that perhaps this would be the best course of action, since Manuel's academic difficulties could indicate a handicapping condition and since there were no other immediate services to which Manuel could be referred.

Dan Singleton, the resource specialist at Sky, tested Manuel and found that although he did have problems understanding vocabulary, he had no auditory, visual, or memory difficulties. Mr. Singleton felt that rather than having a handicapping condition, Manuel simply lacked practice in reading. Mr. Singleton's hypothesis received support when, by reviewing Manuel's records, he discovered that Manuel had attended 10 schools in his short school career and that the main language spoken in the home was Spanish. Manuel had received all his instruction in English and had not received English as a second language services, perhaps because his facility with spoken English masked his limited vocabulary and comprehension.

At the staffing, reports given by other individuals on the committee further supported Mr. Singleton's hypothesis. Manuel's intelligence was determined to be average, and he had no identifiable aural or oral problems. Although he was three grade levels behind in reading (he read at the second-grade level), he was only one grade level behind in math. As the evidence accumulated, it seemed that Manuel's academic problems were not attributable to a handicapping condition. It was also clear, however, that he needed intensive, individual help. This need seemed all the more pressing because Manuel had begun to vent his frustrations in class.

Mr. Singleton has time in his case load and feels sure he can help Manuel if given the chance. However, Manuel cannot be placed in the resource room unless he is found to have a handicapping condition. Because no other special services are available in the building (such as a reading teacher, individual tutoring, etc.), the only option for individualized instruction seems to be the resource room.

Should Manuel be categorized as a special education student?

DISCUSSION. This dilemma seems to revolve around choosing the lesser of two evils: labeling Manuel regardless of whether a handicapping condition can be established versus leaving him without the help he needs. In effect, the staffing committee has to decide whether to "finesse" the federal laws in order to make up for shortcomings of the local resource allocation scheme.

P.L. 94-142 explicitly states that to establish a handicapping condition, an individual's difficulty cannot have been caused by environmental conditions or by cultural or linguistic differences. Because Manuel's is a migrant family that must move often, and because his home language is

Spanish, there is good reason to believe that Manuel satisfies either or both of these particular exclusions in the law. These exclusions were created to avoid the misidentification (labeling) of students with culturally different backgrounds, particularly in schools that have limited services for, and understanding of, students from diverse backgrounds (recall the case, Get My Son Out of Special Education!, p. 48). Given the particulars of this case, if Manuel's difficulties can be traced primarily to the differences between his experiences and those required in school, he cannot be considered "handicapped," in which event it could be a violation of the law to place him in special education.

An important question that arises in this connection is: What constitutes a "real" handicapping condition, particularly a learning disability? There is no doubt that Manuel is having difficulty with reading, and it might be argued that so little is actually known about what constitutes a "real" learning disability, that we might be missing something in Manuel's case. For example, he has difficulty attending to what is happening in class and is struggling with basic reading skills. It is also possible that even if he had had the opportunity to develop literacy skills in his first language, he would still have experienced difficulty. On the other hand, it would seem that there is sufficient evidence regarding Manuel's home and school history to indicate that a lack of consistent, appropriate school experiences and adequate instruction are the likely causes of his difficulties. His file indicates that he has received no specialized help developing his second language skills in English. It also indicates that he has been in all English classrooms, that no particular attention has been given to his status as a second language speaker of English, and that he has consistently been evaluated, erroneously, as a native speaker of English.

As we indicated earlier, research has consistently demonstrated the negative effects of labeling and segregating students into special education classrooms. For students who have a clearly identified handicapping condition, access to specialized help perhaps outweighs these negative effects. Can the same rationale be applied to Manuel's case? One could argue that the long-term consequences of not labeling Manuel would be more severe than those of labeling him without sufficient evidence. It is clear that without special help of some sort Manuel is not going to be adequately prepared to tackle a more advanced curriculum. If he continues to fail in reading, he will be unlikely to succeed in other academic subjects. Furthermore, the dropout rate for Latino students is high, and the chance that Manuel will stay in school decreases as his age increases. Because of his frequent moves, a highly focused, intensive program might be just what Manuel needs. The fact that Manuel has started venting his frustration in school also supports providing intervention immediately. It might be that in a few years his behavior will become so problematic that he could become eligible for special education, but for emotional/behavioral problems. Thus, it can be argued that staffing him into special education would be a "preventative medicine," a strategy that perhaps should be more commonly practiced. Given that there are no other programs in the school that can help him, special education might be viewed as the best alternative to what seems to be a sure academic decline.

What, then, should be done, *all things considered*? We would give the staffing committee different advice. Miramontes takes the position that labeling Manuel when no handicapping condition exists undermines the integrity of special education services and allows the district to abdicate its obligation to address the variety of needs that students have, and to use special education as an all-purpose catch basin for "problem" students. She believes that other services *must* be made available. Approaching the problem from a different perspective, she raises the issue of why, if one accepts the position that the resource specialist's intervention is to be seen as "preventative," prevention should not be applied *before* labeling rather than after? If the rules can be bent in one direction (labeling without clearly establishing a handicapping condition), why can't they be bent in the other direction (letting the resource specialist work with a student who is clearly in need, without labeling)? Howe, on the other hand, believes that the stakes are too high to take a stand on "the principle" of the matter and to wait until some new set of practices and services can be negotiated (although he agrees that such changes are clearly needed). With regard to labeling, Howe believes that, on balance, Manuel will be harmed more by not getting the academic help he needs immediately than by being labeled learning disabled. Howe believes that the label "LD" is much less stigmatizing than other labels such as "EBD," "MR," and so forth.

PROFESSIONAL RELATIONSHIPS

More than in other areas of public education, special education requires a high degree of teamwork and cooperation because of the requirement for IEPs as well as the move toward integration. As a consequence, the problems that are engendered by close working relationships, including the possibility for friction and conflict among various professionals, are more frequent and more magnified than in public education more generally.

The need to establish close working relationships can lead to biases in judgment that cut in both directions. On the one hand, it can be easy to overlook the shortcomings of a co-worker where he or she is likeable. Special circumstances such as personal hardships—financial difficulties, marital problems, a person who has beaten the odds—also pull one toward making special allowances. (Here, one tends to overlook the interests of the affected students.) On the other hand, co-workers who are not likeable or, for whatever reason, seem to deserve no special consideration too easily prompt one to be particularly harsh, perhaps to the point of forgoing normal procedures of due process. (Here, one tends to take the interests of the affected children very seriously.)

Matters are further complicated by the previously mentioned utilitarian stance that institutions so frequently take—the "putting out fires" mentality. In particular, school administrations are often reluctant to take on the task of disciplining or dismissing educational personnel, even when they seem to be failing to discharge their responsibilities in an acceptable manner. In light of due process protections, particularly tenure, such attempts are typically perceived as causing too much stress, embarrassment, and expense for the institution, as well as being an all-around hassle. In light of these attitudes, individuals involved in special education are frequently faced with situations in which they must find some way to work closely with co-workers who are unproductive or worse. They may also be required to take up the slack created by those who fail to effectively perform their duties.

Case: Covering for Incompetence

George Hendricks, a certified school social worker, was assigned, along with a school psychologist and a resource teacher, to the case of Michael Clark, a sixth grader at Morningdale Elementary School. Something was obstructing Michael's educational and social progress. Additionally, Michael's misbehavior was interfering with the learning of his classmates. Thus, the team, along with his classroom teacher, believed that Michael should be evaluated for a suspected emotional disturbance.

In a pre-evaluation meeting the tasks of each member were agreed upon. The team decided that thorough documentation was important in order to help convince Michael's parents of the need for a full evaluation and staffing. The classroom teacher was requested to keep a diary; other team members were asked to do an informal but systematic and well-documented evaluation. The team agreed to reconvene to analyze the data prior to making the required home visit or suggesting a course of action to the principal.

This data gathering was considered "delicate" because Michael's parents felt that the school continually singled them and Michael out as targets for embarrassment and rebuke. This perception was aggravated by the fact that pressure was also being placed on the family by social services to approve Michael's evaluation. Thus, the pre-evaluation team believed that in order to prevent further alienation, sensitivity to the family's concerns was of utmost importance.

An additional problem in this case was that Mr. Hendricks, the social worker in charge of home visits, had not handled sensitive situations well in the past, and the other team members did not trust his ability to do so in this case. Thus, the team eschewed the standard procedure of having a single member do a home visit as a first step, and instead decided to develop a better argument in support of a full evaluation as the first step, and then to have a pair from the team do the home visit with the parents. By using this strategy, they hoped to be able to handle the situation much more sensitively than if they left the task to Mr. Hendricks alone.

Mr. Hendricks scuttled the plan: When he completed his observations, he reported his findings directly to the principal and asked whether he could make the home visit. Following standard procedure, the principal approved the request. After getting their consent, Mr. Hendricks made a home visit to the Clark family. Predictably, the visit resulted in a heated exchange between Mr. Hendricks and Michael's parents. Mr. Hendricks told the parents that Michael was emotionally disturbed and needed to be placed in a special classroom. The parents told Mr. Hendricks they would never give permission for an evaluation of Michael and that they were sick of the school's interference in their affairs. The reaction of the other members of the team to Mr. Hendricks' actions was "He did it again!"

Team members were frustrated by the frequent need to repair the damage done by Mr. Hendricks and wanted to exclude him, but had to defer to the district guidelines, which required that a social worker serve on evaluation teams. Numerous efforts to help Mr. Hendricks realize the consequences of his actions and poorly chosen words typically yielded an "Oh, I'm sorry." When his missteps were brought to the attention of his supervisor, they were greeted with "I'll talk to him about it." But things didn't change.

Eventually, a more expedient way to complete evaluations and to relieve Mr. Hendricks of a major part of his responsibility was suggested by the school psychologist. Even though other team members lacked the specific expertise and credentials of a certified social worker, they believed they could do a better job than Mr. Hendricks. Therefore, Mr. Hendricks could simply be asked to review the reports and sign them, indicating agreement (a situation that everyone felt he would welcome).

Should this way of dealing with Mr. Hendricks be adopted? What are the alternatives?

DISCUSSION. The first question that arises in this case is why the principal wasn't brought in on the plan. Had the principal been involved, it would have been highly unlikely that Mr. Hendricks could have scuttled the plan in the way he did and further alienated the parents in the process. Perhaps the principal is generally uninvolved in the workings of special education in the school, and perhaps this helps explain Mr. Hendricks' performance. In any case, the problem is larger than this isolated event, which explains the suggestion that others take over Mr. Hendricks' responsibility to conduct home visits. We will consider this suggestion shortly, after first exploring several other options.

One option would be to try to have Mr. Hendricks fired. But this seems a bit drastic, at least at this point. For it appears that Mr. Hendricks himself has not been duly informed of his inadequate performance (only his supervisor has) and that no genuine attempts have been made to help him improve. Thus, attempting to have him fired not only is likely to fail for procedural reasons, but it also seems unfair to not give him a chance. This suggests that it might be a good idea to try to set the wheels in motion that could eventually lead to Mr. Hendricks' firing, but only after he has been informed and has had an adequate opportunity to improve. The success of such a strategy would hinge on the cooperation of his supervisor, who so far has proven quite unwilling to do anything substantive about the situation. For this reason, it could prove necessary to try to take action higher in the chain of authority.

Another option would be to suggest that Mr. Hendricks be reassigned to a position that wouldn't require home visits (admittedly a somewhat odd suggestion to make with respect to a social worker, who has been trained to help people deal with their problems). This, too, would require the cooperation of Mr. Hendricks' supervisor or someone else with the necessary authority. Its feasibility would depend on a host of other factors as well, particularly whether any positions for social workers existed and were open that did not include home visits among their responsibilities.

If neither of these options worked, a third option would be to try to have Mr. Hendricks "turfed" somewhere else, so that the staff at Morningdale would no longer have to deal with him. Perhaps his supervisor would be more receptive to this strategy. Though tempting (and probably widely practiced in a variety of contexts), this strategy simply lays the problem at others', including children's, doorsteps. Therefore, it is a strategy we do not endorse.

This leads to the suggestion made by the school psychologist: to have someone else do the home visits and have Mr. Hendricks simply do the necessary paper work. This strategy, it seems, would solve the major problems, but it has several drawbacks. First, it seems to amount to breaking the letter of the law (i.e., district policy), which requires that home visits be conducted by a certified social worker. It thus not only involves certain risks, but could be blocked by individuals in authority. Second, it has to be galling for other members of the team to have to assume additional responsibilities without being recognized or rewarded for such an undertaking. Ironically, this strategy rewards incompetence with a lighter work load, and competence with a heavier one.

All things considered, we would endorse a stepwise procedure. First, Mr. Hendricks and his supervisor should be approached by the team, and their concerns should be driven home and not permitted to be sloughed off. Second, an attempt should be made to establish the procedures and criteria for improving George's performance and determining whether they have been successful; the consequences of failure to improve should also be specified, for example, discharge, demotion, and so forth. Third, if the second step cannot be accomplished, then it seems there is no alternative to taking the school psychologist's suggestion.

Case: Turfing Students

Anne Davies taught in a self-contained special education classroom; her friend Beth Grant also taught in a self-contained classroom. Each had 10 students and a full-time aide. Whereas Ms. Davies' classroom was devoted to students with educable mental retardation, Ms. Grant had only students with severe multiple handicaps in her classroom. Ms. Grant confided in Ms. Davies that she really liked this type of classroom because she didn't have to worry about academic skills and wasn't held accountable for fostering them. Although her students required a good deal of attention, she thought they were overall quite easy to manage.

Due to changes in district policy, Ms. Grant's classroom was changed so that there was a wider range of academic ability among her students. Unlike in previous years, she now also had students for whom she felt academically accountable. Although as part of the new policy, Ms. Grant had two fewer students, she did not like the arrangement and thought it was a double load. She was especially unhappy about one student in particular, Vu. Vu had severe, multiple physical handicaps as well as a catheter that required careful, specialized attention throughout the day. Although Vu had been in Ms. Grant's class the year before, which made it possible for him to remain in his neighborhood school,

Ms. Grant wanted him transferred elsewhere. She believed that with the change in policy her range of responsibilities within the classroom had become too broad, and she voiced her concerns to her supervisor. She also suggested to Ms. Davies that perhaps Vu could be accommodated in her classroom.

Although Ms. Davies believed that Vu would probably have a better experience in her classroom, given Ms. Grant's attitude, she reminded her friend that she had no training or experience with Vu's medical condition. She also pointed out that a transfer would require a long daily trip for him, and that if he were removed from his neighborhood school, his parents would no longer be close by in case of an emergency. In addition, since Vu's parents did not speak much English, it would be harder for them to make the necessary arrangements for him to attend a distant school; furthermore, they had previously stated their wish that Vu attend his neighborhood school.

To her dismay, one Wednesday afternoon Ms. Davies received a slip from the central special education office informing her that Vu would be arriving in her class the next Monday. She immediately called the office to talk to her supervisor, Jane Akima, about the transfer and found that she had been out of town until that morning and knew nothing about it. Evidently, the transfer had been arranged by Ms. Grant and her supervisor, Martha Villa, without consulting either Ms. Davies or Ms. Akima.

Upon questioning by Ms. Akima, Ms. Villa explained that Ms. Grant had been insistent about her inability to deal with Vu in light of the new makeup of her classroom. Out of concern for Vu's welfare, and in an effort to expedite matters, Ms. Villa had made the decision to transfer Vu to Ms. Davies' classroom.

What should Ms. Davies do?

DISCUSSION. It would appear that some sort of procedural breakdown occurred in order for the transfer of Vu to have happened, especially since Ms. Davies and Ms. Akima supported keeping Vu in his neighborhood school. Perhaps this incident is merely an instance of one hand not knowing what the other hand is doing. Given Ms. Grant's attitude, her supervisor seems to have been motivated by the feeling that Vu could be better served in a different setting. Trying to expedite matters, she moved ahead to alleviate the problem without fully considering the consequences for all involved. If proper procedures were violated in the process, Vu might simply be returned to Ms. Grant's classroom, and the reason for first transferring and then returning Vu to his home school would have to be explained to his parents.

Even if the case could be resolved in this way, what gave rise to it in the first place raises more fundamental questions that are worthy of attention in their own right. Consider Ms. Grant's position. On the one hand, she might be perceived as wishing to assume only a caretaker role with the students in her classroom. This raises the question of whether she embraces a view of special education associated with "warehousing" and "turfing" children who have severe learning difficulties, as opposed to a view of special education associated with responding to the special needs of students in order that they might be prepared to enjoy the highest quality of life of which they are capable. (If she holds the former view, whether she should be in special education is open to serious question.)

On the other hand, this perception of Ms. Grant may be unwarranted. Apparently, her mix of students was changed due to a new district policy that she had nothing to do with formulating. It is altogether possible that her job has been made more demanding by the new policy. If so, she may well have a legitimate concern that should be addressed. In general, there ought to be some way to determine what a fair load of students is, and this determination ought to include, as far as possible, the particular mix of students that are assigned to given special education teachers.

These other issues aside, the manner in which Ms. Grant and Ms. Villa went about having Vu transferred appears open to criticism. Rather than pursuing the matter in an explicit and aboveboard way, they chose to instigate the transfer without informing either Ms. Davies or Ms. Akima. This makes one wonder whether Ms. Grant wasn't trying to exploit her friendship with Ms. Davies, trusting that she would not complain. Furthermore, Ms. Grant apparently also ignored the wishes of Vu's parents with her surreptitious method. This seems to be an especial problem insofar as Vu's parents are an ethnic minority who speak little English and thus are probably relatively poorly equipped to assert their interests.

CHAPTER 5

Students and Parents as Sources of Obligation

In this chapter we examine ethical problems associated with "the view from here." Our focus will be on situations in which the welfare of particular students and their parents are at stake and in which individual special educators have the greatest power to shape the immediate course of events. The cases will focus on ethical deliberation within the "elbow room" permitted by institutional and broader policy constraints.

Parental involvement in determining a special education student's educational program is specifically mandated in P.L. 94–142. Such parental participation not only serves to provide due process protections, but research on children with both severe and mild handicaps indicates that parental involvement enhances the chances of academic success of special education students. On the other hand, teachers may find that their own values, professional judgment, and program implementation may be at odds with the vision of education parents see for their children. On occasion, parents' desires with regard to the education of their children may also be at odds with the intent of the law. Again, there is no substitute for careful ethical deliberation.

CONFLICTS AMONG PARENTS AND TEACHERS ABOUT STUDENT WELFARE

In the U.S. public school system, citizens in general, and parents in particular, have a rather large voice in the conduct of education. Such a voice is rooted in principles of local control and parental autonomy (the right of parents to raise their children consistent with their own values). Furthermore, active parental participation is endorsed by educators—inside and outside of schools—as a means of improving the effectiveness of education. Finally, and with regard to special education in particular, parental participation is mandated through the vehicle of IEPs.

Not surprisingly, participation by parents inevitably leads to conflicts between educators and parents about what is best for the education of children. These conflicts can take different forms—about the content of the curriculum, about whether special education students should be subject to the same grading standards as other students, about mainstreaming, and so forth—and they sometimes place individual teachers between individual parents and their children in such a way that the teacher must in some sense attempt to protect a child. Child abuse and neglect are common examples, but frequently there are also less extreme situations that call for careful deliberation.

Case: Withholding Information About Poor Performance?

James is in the fifth grade. In second grade it was determined that he had a learning disability, a perceptual problem that interfered with his ability to read. For the past year-and-a-half he has been receiving resource room help for 2 hours a day and has been able to hold his own, although he has struggled with the reading load in the content areas. This year James' difficulties are making it increasingly difficult for him to keep up with his schoolwork. At the first-quarter reporting period Ms. Hays, James' resource teacher, met with his mother, Ms. Jones, and explained to her that the increased reading load in fifth grade was making it difficult for James to complete his work during class time. She requested that Ms. Jones give James help and encouragement at home. Ms. Jones agreed. After several weeks, however, James' work had not improved and his behavior had begun to change. He became less and less willing to try anything new and was concerned only with whether his work was correct. He was very anxious about any work in which errors had been indicated by the teacher, and he insisted that he be allowed to write corrected versions to take home.

James was in the regular education classroom for social studies, and Ms. Hays had always believed that it was important for him to take tests with the rest of the class and to otherwise be evaluated in the same way as his peers, so that he would be prepared for his subsequent education. Unfortunately, he usually performed quite poorly. One day following one of the social studies tests on which James received a low grade his behavior took a noticeable turn for the worse. He became extremely anxious and reluctant to complete his work. Ms. Hays was concerned, and called James' home. James' father answered and she proceeded to tell him about her concerns regarding James' inability to keep up with his schoolwork and the effect it was having on his behavior. Ms. Hays got an unhappy surprise when James' father became angry and said he was convinced that all concerned had been too lenient with James. After all, he reasoned, hadn't James been getting extra help for over 2 years? He went on to say that he had been brought up to believe that hard work and perseverance were the ways to overcome obstacles. Although he knew James was identified as having a learning disability, he was convinced that James just needed to try harder. He told Ms. Hays that he had been cracking down on James and that James had gotten a spanking for his poor showing on the last social studies test. Mr. Jones assured Ms. Hays that he would continue such punishment as long as James didn't improve.

Ms. Hays was dismayed. The last thing she thought James needed was discouragement and having his anxiety about school work exacerbated. She also objected in principle to spanking as a form of punishment.

What should Ms. Hays do?

DISCUSSION. Ms. Hays' first step should be to investigate Mr. and Ms. Jones's history in dealing with James and the schools, which would include seeking out the advice and knowledge of individuals such as other teachers, counselors, social workers, and the school principal. Also, Ms. Hays should contact Ms. Jones to see whether she and her husband agree. Ultimately, it might be a good idea for Ms. Hays to arrange a conference with Mr. and Ms. Jones (and whatever other individuals seem appropriate) to try to convince Mr. Jones to be less punitive with James.

The disagreement between Ms. Hays and Mr. Jones about James implicitly raises a fundamental philosophical issue that permeates the institution of special education, namely, the potential conflict between what may be termed "therapeutic" and "moral" perspectives on learning and behavioral difficulties. (We discussed similar issues under the rubric of the "bureau-therapeutic" structure of special education in Chapter 3, and particularly in connection with the case, Delinquent or Disturbed?, p. 32.) Put in the simplest terms, a therapeutic perspective focuses on the concept of *disability* for which individuals are not responsible and for which they require therapy or special compensating treatment (attributing learning disabilities to a hearing impairment or to dyslexia are paradigms that fit this perspective); a moral perspective focuses on *character traits* for which individuals are responsible and for which they deserve blame for failing to measure up (attributing learning difficulties to laziness or to defiance of authority are paradigms that fit this perspective). Ms. Hays leans toward the therapeutic perspective, and Mr. Jones leans toward the moral perspective. Trying to convince Mr. Jones that his perspective is mistaken would require challenging some of his fundamental beliefs, and thus would probably be doomed to failure. On the other hand, Ms. Hays ought to take Mr. Jones' beliefs into account in her dealings with him and try to get him to moderate them. She could suggest to Mr. Jones that James does seem to be trying hard (in answer to Mr. Jones' suspicion about James' character) and that blaming and spanking James for poor performance are likely to be ineffective.

If Ms. Hays fails to reach a satisfactory agreement with Mr. and Ms. Jones, then she is faced with the difficult decision of whether to try to protect James from his father. For example, regarding the work James takes home, she could select only his best efforts or allow him to create corrected versions. Although this strategy might protect James from his father, it has the undesirable feature of deceiving James' parents (as well as making James a part of the deception). Perhaps the deception might be justified, but it appears that the consequences are such that it would simply lead to further problems down the road. If James' parents were led to believe that all was well with James' schoolwork, they would be less inclined to give him the help he needs at home. Furthermore, James will ultimately receive grading period reports that presumably will reflect the overall quality of his work. Thus, unless Ms. Hays falsified James' grade, the deception would be discovered sooner or later and would make matters worse for all involved than being consistently honest would.

Provided that Ms. Hays doesn't simply give James higher grades than his work merits in order to keep him out of trouble at home, she seems forced to re-examine her grading policies, in particular whether James (and perhaps other students like him) should be evaluated in the same way as other students in social studies. We would suggest that she consider tailoring her evaluations (as part of James' IEP) in a way that takes into account James' particular learning difficulties. In one of the cases in this chapter (Special Grading for Special Education Students?, p. 93) we will consider the issue of grading in detail.

Case: Parents' Wishes Versus Professional Judgment

Helen Burns teaches in a kindergarten classroom for students with severe intellectual difficulties. She is a strong advocate of integration and has worked hard to forge an alliance with a regular education classroom teacher to integrate her students. She has worked out an arrangement with one of the regular kindergarten teachers such that her class spends an hour-and-a-half daily involved in regular education classroom activities. The two classes also share special occasions together, such as holiday parties. Ms. Burns is very proud of the arrangement and of the growth she has seen in both groups of students since they began working together.

Rosie James is a student in Ms. Burns' class. She is a sweet and happy child, and many of the students in the regular class seek her out as a playmate and companion. Ms. Burns makes a home visit to the parents of each of her students twice a year. When she visited with Rosie's mother, Ms. Burns enthusiastically explained her integration program and described the types of activities Rosie was engaged in and the opportunities it opened for her. Ms. James listened attentively and politely, so Ms. Burns was not prepared for Ms. James' response that she did not want Rosie to be a part of the program.

Ms. James explained that in her childhood she had a friend who was mentally retarded. Her friend was fine when she and Ms. James played at home and she was fine in her special classes at school, but at school outside her special classes she was taunted and humiliated on several occasions. When they entered junior high school, her friend was put into some of the regular classes and here Ms. James had witnessed firsthand how cruelly she was treated. As a result of the experiences of her childhood friend, Ms. James felt very strongly about not putting Rosie in situations that would make her vulnerable to the same kind of taunting and humiliation that her friend had undergone.

Although she acknowledged the importance of Ms. James' personal experience, Ms. Burns believed that it did not apply to Rosie's situation. Ms. Burns believes that schools are changing and that integration provides children with many opportunities not open to them in other ways. She also believes that children with handicapping conditions cannot be sheltered forever. Instead, they must learn to interact with the wider community and, in turn, the community must learn to interact with them.

Ms. Burns had invested a great deal of time designing and implementing the integration program. The results she saw with the class as a whole gave her great satisfaction and further reinforced her belief that integration was the principle that should guide special education. Furthermore, Rosie could not be left alone when the rest of the class, along with Ms. Burns, went to the regular classroom. Thus, unless Ms. Burns were to completely change her program, Rosie had to be included in it at some level. Ms. Burns tried to accommodate Ms. James' wishes (though somewhat halfheartedly) by minimizing Rosie's interactions with other students.

On Halloween the two classes had a joint party in the regular classroom. All the parents were invited and Ms. James attended. Because Rosie was popular with many of the children, they freely talked with her and invited her to participate in their games. After watching quietly for a few minutes, Ms. James pulled Rosie aside and then kept her separated from the children's activities. Ms. Burns' attention was focused on other things for the remainder of the afternoon and she didn't have the opportunity to talk with Ms. James before she left.

What should Ms. Burns do now?

DISCUSSION. Ms. Burns is faced with the following dilemma: On the one hand, it is her responsibility to provide a program that coincides with the legal requirement to place students in the least restrictive environment. She also agrees with this requirement in spirit and has her personal experience to attest to its feasibility and positive effects. On the other hand, there is also the legal requirement that parents of special needs children be directly involved in negotiating their child's IEP, and it is clear that Ms. James does not want Rosie to participate in the integration activities being provided.

In the face of this tension between requirements, Ms. Burns continued to include Rosie in the integration program, while making a halfhearted attempt to appease Ms. James. Ordinarily, this might have been sufficient to resolve the tension and to permit Ms. Burns to carry on with her regular routine. But this case is not ordinary. Rosie is an outgoing, popular, and happy child. Children in the regular program seek her out and enjoy her company. Thus, Rosie's and the other children's behavior at the Halloween party, as well as Ms. James' response, were quite predictable.

Ms. James' response to the Halloween party might have been different if Ms. Burns had pursued the issues more carefully with her following their initial difference of opinion about including Rosie in the integration program—her halfhearted compromise obviously didn't work. Suppose that Ms. Burns had convinced Ms. James to at least take a wait and see attitude regarding including Rosie in the integration program in order to determine whether Rosie might have a completely different experience from Ms. James' childhood friend, as Ms. Burns believed she would have. If such a compromise had been negotiated, then the Halloween party could have served as an opportunity to test out this hypothesis and, given the manner in which the other children responded to Rosie, it might have convinced Ms. James that the integration program was indeed beneficial to Rosie.

Since the party has already occurred, Ms. Burns' position is weakened—both because Rosie was precluded from full participation in the party by Ms. James and because Ms. James' opposition to including Rosie in the integration program may have stiffened in light of the way Ms. Burns apparently ignored her wishes. Nonetheless, it appears that Ms. Burns can no longer get by with halfhearted measures or with avoiding direct negotiations with Ms. James.

Ms. Burns might start by asking Ms. James to reflect on what she saw at the Halloween party and whether Rosie was being taunted and humiliated as she feared. She could also ask Ms. James to reflect on the fact that integration is the norm in Rosie's school, and point out that the possible effects on Rosie of including her in the regular classroom but excluding her from participation with the other children might cause Rosie to be viewed in exactly the way Ms. James fears. Might Rosie not be perceived as unfriendly and different by the other students in the class? If left out of the group's activities, might she not herself begin to feel excluded and unliked and begin to withdraw? Finally, Ms. Burns could try to convince Ms. James that the world has changed since she was a child and that integration programs are making it possible for a mutual understanding to develop among children who have a diverse range of abilities. She could reiterate her strong belief that Rosie will have a fuller, more satisfying life if she is able to learn to live in the world at large, not just within the sheltered environment of her home, and that someday she will have to.

Beyond this, there seems little more that Ms. Burns can do. In the end, she might have to, regrettably, "wash her hands" of the situation—in the interests of her integrity, the integrity of the program, and the interests of other children—and suggest that Ms. James arrange a different placement for Rosie. Ms. Burns can no longer employ her middle of the road, halfhearted approach.

CONFIDENTIALITY

Protecting confidentiality is a principle that has been defended in fields such as medical ethics on both utilitarian and non-consequentialist grounds. The basic arguments may be extended to education in a rather straightforward way. The utilitarian justification would be that unless confidentiality is protected, students will not come forward with their problems and thus cannot be provided with the help they may need; the non-consequentialist justification would be that in order to show respect for students, individuals who exist in a trusting relationship with them (which presumably is required for effective teaching and counseling) must not publicize what is told to them in confidence.

Regardless of which one of these general justifications one finds more convincing (if either), protecting confidentiality is complicated by at least two considerations when those whose confidentiality is at issue are children: justified paternalism and family autonomy. Regarding justified paternalism, because children are typically not mature enough to be afforded full autonomy and privacy (though, of course, individual situations can be very difficult to judge) adults standing in various relationships to them (parents, teachers, physicians, and so forth) may have to override the expressed wishes of children, including that certain information be kept confidential, for their own best interests. Regarding family autonomy, our society grants a wide area of discretion to parents to raise their children as they see fit, such that parents can demand that they be provided with information they deem relevant to raising or protecting their children that their children or school personnel would rather keep confidential (again, individual situations can be very difficult to judge).

Viewed from another perspective, however, these general kinds of arguments cannot be so easily extended to education. Unlike other professions (e.g., law and medicine), teachers do not share an historical commitment to protecting confidentiality. Information about students is often freely (probably too freely) shared in schools, to the point where individual students (as well as whole families) sometimes acquire reputations captured in remarks such as "Oh, you have Carl Jenkins this year, good luck!"

For special education teachers, maintaining the confidentiality of students and their families can be a constant worry. Because special education teachers often work with fewer students, and more closely, students frequently share intimate information about themselves, their families, and friends. In order to obtain the cooperation and understanding of regular classroom teachers, some of this information must be divulged. Insofar as the general school environment lacks articulated norms and guidelines about the teacher–student relationship, the special educator's task in dealing with sensitive information is all the more difficult.

Case: Loose Talk in the Lounge

Susan Agar, the resource teacher at Hilltop Junior High School, had been working with Linda, a fifth grader with a hearing impairment, for several months when Linda became withdrawn and uncooperative. As a result of a conversation with the school nurse, Ms. Agar learned that the nurse suspected Linda had been the recent victim of sexual abuse. There was no conclusive evidence, however, and Linda was unwilling to talk about it, even when questioned directly by the nurse. The nurse reminded Ms. Agar that it was a very sensitive matter and should be handled discreetly.

Ms. Agar had never been involved in such a case before and was therefore anxious to talk with other staff members about how she should approach Linda. She also believed that Linda's other teachers should be made aware of the possible cause of Linda's recent behavior changes so that they might be understanding and supportive as well as alert to any evidence that might help document the suspected sexual abuse.

Because of her very busy school schedule, Ms. Agar had difficulty finding an opportunity to discuss Linda's situation with the other teachers. One day at lunch, however, she found several of Linda's teachers together and took this opportunity to raise the issue. Because it was a very sensitive matter, Ms. Agar did not mention Linda's name. Over the course of the conversation, however, Linda's name eventually came up. Several of Linda's teachers had noticed a marked change in her behavior; but, not being privy to the nurse's suspicions, they believed Linda had simply become a trouble maker and were preparing to take disciplinary action against her. The discussion became quite heated and Linda's family was discussed at length.

The teachers' lounge was a busy place where many teachers congregated. Because it was near the workroom, teachers' aides and parent volunteers were frequently within earshot. Ms. Agar realized that several other people, including two parents, had overheard the discussion. Although she was glad that Linda's other teachers had been made aware of the possible cause of Linda's changed behavior, she wondered whether Linda's and her family's confidentiality had been violated. She also began to regret having brought the subject up in so public a context and began to think she should have kept the whole thing to herself.

Did Ms. Agar do the right thing? What should she do now?

DISCUSSION. As we suggested earlier, because of their relatively more intimate relationship with their students, which flows from the need to know the precise nature of special needs students' difficulties, the formulation of IEPs, and so forth, special education teachers often come to know a great deal about special needs students, including the details of these students' personal lives. As a consequence, they often face questions of how much of this more intimate knowledge to share, and with whom. An additional question is the means by which such information should be shared.

In the present case, Ms. Agar's decision to raise the issue in the teachers' lounge led to difficulties regarding all three of these questions. Although she may not have been able to foresee the precise outcome of her means—a rather heated discussion that could easily be overheard—the general environment of the teachers' lounge is not conducive to discussing such sensitive issues. Even if the discussion hadn't taken the shape it did, teachers' lounges are centers of information networks (if not outright gossip) such that it is virtually impossible to prevent private information from circulating more widely than it should. Thus, even if the discussion had not become heated, it could have been anticipated from the environment of the teachers' lounge that individuals would find out about Linda's suspected abuse who shouldn't have found out, and that more information would be revealed about Linda's family (in the form of various teachers' opinions) than should have been revealed. As a consequence, Linda and her family clearly seem to have been wronged, especially since the nurse's suspicions could prove to be unfounded. Furthermore, even if the suspicions proved to be true, this much information should not have been revealed to this many people.

But what should Ms. Agar do now, after the incident of the teachers' lounge discussion? She might simply do nothing and hope the incident has no consequences of note. A better alternative in our estimation is for Ms. Agar to do what she can to contain the situation. Specifically, she should talk to the individuals involved, either individually or in a group, regarding her concerns about the breach of confidentiality for Linda and her family. She should encourage these individuals to keep the discussion to themselves and remind them of the possibility that the suspicions of sexual abuse could be unfounded and that, in any case, this is not something that should become public knowledge.

We do not mean to suggest that Ms. Agar could have no jusitification for sharing sensitive, confidential information about Linda. In particular, schools function (and should function) as teams, such that otherwise private information about students is shared among the staff in order to best meet students' needs. As we suggested earlier, special education teachers have a special role and obligation in this regard. On the other hand, as we also suggested earlier, the means of communicating information, how much is communicated, and to whom, have to be carefully considered in order to ensure that the risks of undesirable consequences to students and their parents are minimized. Ms. Agar should have given these considerations a good deal more attention.

Case: Who Really Needs to Know?

Steven Smith is a seventeen-year-old junior at Jefferson High School, a large high school (enrollment slightly over 2,000), located in Riverdale, a midwestern industrial city with a population of 150,000.

In the middle of the fall semester, after Steven had been absent for several days, Mr. Jenkins, the principal at Jefferson, received a phone call from Steven's mother, who was quite distraught. The reason for her distress soon became clear: Steven had been diagnosed as having AIDS

Related Complex (or ARC), a syndrome that has some of the same symptoms as AIDS (for example, fever, vomiting, and weakness) and that is often a precursor of AIDS. (Steven apparently contracted the virus as the result of a massive blood transfusion he had received several years earlier in the course of being treated for injuries sustained in an auto accident.) Ms. Smith wants Steven to return to school, but she also wants his condition kept confidential. After further discussion, she agreed that Mr. Donnelly, the special education teacher, should be informed of Steven's condition. The ARC diagnosis would probably entitle Steven to special education services under the classification "chronic illness"; if so, Mr. Donnelly would be working closely with him and would need this information to interpret Steven's academic progress and to understand the frequent absences that could be anticipated. Steven's mother insisted that no one else be told. Following his conversation with Ms. Smith, Mr. Jenkins told Mr. Donnelly about Steven's condition.

The school district had developed a policy on AIDS (the result of a compromise between those who wanted full disclosure and those who wanted none) according to which parents and teachers would be informed when a student infected with the AIDS virus was attending school but the particular student would not be identified. Up to this point, the policy had worked effectively; several students had been permitted to attend several schools without incident.

Things changed at Jefferson. When Mr. Jenkins told a group of teachers and parents he had assembled that an AIDS-infected student would be attending Jefferson, there was a huge outcry and a demand that the student be identified. Parents pointed out that the previous cases in which the policy had worked all involved elementary school children and argued that things were different when it came to high schoolers. In particular, they claimed that they needed to know who the infected student was in order to protect their children from routes of transmission such as athletics (particularly football and wrestling) and sex. Several teachers were in agreement with the parents, and they went on to add that they needed to know in order to effectively teach the student in question. Some teachers were insulted: They wondered why they should be kept in the dark when the principal knew. Were they supposed to just "follow orders" issued from the "bosses on mount high"? Were they not to be trusted?

What position and action should Mr. Donnelly take? Who, if anyone, beyond Mr. Jenkins and Mr. Donnelly should know Steven's condition?

DISCUSSION. A useful principle for determining whether and to whom otherwise private information should be revealed is the "need to know." This principle can be justified on the grounds both that in certain circumstances it is in the best interests of the person whose confidentiality is being compromised (for instance, in order to provide the best care, an emergency room physician might obtain the medical history of an unconscious accident victim from a relative) and that in other circumstances a person's confidentiality has to be traded off against the interests of others (for instance, a psychiatrist whose patient reveals a plan to commit murder has a "duty to warn" the individual whose life is threatened).

In the present case, the parents and certain teachers invoke the latter justification for why they need to know; Mr. Jenkins invokes the former for why Mr. Donnelly needs to know. From Mr. Donnelly's standpoint, because he is the special education teacher, private information fell into his lap as a result of his close working relationship with his students and of Mr. Jenkins' decision to tell him. He knows of Steven's condition and is now faced with the question of what to do about it in the face of the controversy at Jefferson.

In our estimation, the district policy is a good one (though we are not sure that the "compromise," informing the public when an AIDS-infected child is attending a given school, makes good sense) and should be adhered to in this case. Without getting into the details of issues of confidentiality regarding AIDS-infected school children (but see, for example, Reed, 1988; Howe, 1990), the risks are often vastly overestimated and the harm to those infected individuals whose confidentiality is breached is often underestimated (a family in Arcadia, Florida was burned out of their home when the community learned that two boys, both hemophiliacs, who were attending a local school were infected with the AIDS virus; Reed, 1988). Furthermore, the fact that Steven is in school should not serve as a pretext for denying him rights of confidentiality that he would otherwise have (regarding health insurance, employment, and so forth). In short, we believe that parents and teachers do not have a good case in support of a "need to know" on the grounds of risks to themselves and their children, especially in light of the possible harmful consequences for Steven. Accordingly, Mr. Donnelly should not respond to this argument.

This leaves open the other kind of "need to know" argument: that it would be in Steven's best interests for others (at least some others) to know of his condition. Mr. Jenkins and Mr. Donnelly already know on these grounds. Should Mr. Donnelly advocate informing additional individuals?

Ideally, it would be desirable to convince the school staff and parents that the only legitimate basis for a "need to know" which particular school children are infected with the AIDS virus was in order to respond to such children's needs. (This premise is reflected in policy recommendations of bodies such as the Centers for Disease Control and presumably went into the formulation of the district policy.) Reaching such an agreement, Mr. Donnelly and Mr. Jenkins could then proceed to tell those individuals working directly with Steven (for instance, the individuals involved in determining Steven's IEP) about his condition, emphasizing the need to strictly maintain Steven's confidentiality. This strategy would have the advantage of providing individuals who work with Steven information that would help account for the possibility of frequent absences, declining achievement, and other behavioral changes such as depression. It might also assuage those teachers who believe information is being withheld from them arbitrarily.

This strategy would not necessarily require getting all, or even a majority, of teachers and parents to agree, though it would certainly make things better if they did. If they didn't, Mr. Jenkins could simply fall back on the district policy and insist that it be followed. On the other hand, the strategy *would* require that those individuals to be told, beyond Mr. Jenkins and Mr. Donnelly, could be trusted, which would depend on the kinds of individuals they were, a judgment that would be up to Mr. Donnelly and Mr. Jenkins to make. In the end, it might be wise for Steven to forgo special education services if the prospect of discussing his condition in order to formulate an IEP was too threatening. In this connection, the view of Steven's mother would have to be taken quite seriously, because she trusts both Mr. Jenkins and Mr. Donnelly and because Mr. Jenkins promised her that no one else would be told. Finally, Steven himself should be heard, since he is at the center of the problem and has the most to gain or lose. At 17 years old, his views should surely carry considerable weight.

SPECIAL ALLOWANCES FOR SPECIAL EDUCATION STUDENTS?

In previous chapters we treated issues such as the special education teacher's responsibility to broker for services for special education students, unequal power within IEP staffings, and related issues having to do with advocacy. These kinds of problems often have to do with conflicts *between* the interests of special and regular education students. We will consider one more case in this vein, which has to do with grading, an activity (too infrequently examined carefully) where individual teachers have rather wide latitude. On the other hand, conflicts may also occur *within* the arena of special education, presenting special educators with the problem of ensuring that special education students are treated appropriately vis-à-vis other special education students. The second case in this section will deal with various aspects of this issue.

Case: Special Grading for Special Education Students?

Bob Hartpence is the ninth-grade Biology I teacher at Emerson High School. It is the end of the year and time to assign grades, and every student at Emerson must take and pass Biology I to graduate. Mr. Hartpence employs the following grading scheme: two-fifths of the grade for the first half of the semester, two-fifths for the second half of the semester, and one-fifth for the final examination. Students need an average of at least 50% to pass.

Anne Padilla, the special education teacher, team taught with Bob over the year, collaborating on John, a student with learning disabilities. John failed the first half of the semester with a 39%. He worked very hard the second half to improve his grade. Mr. Hartpence and Ms. Padilla helped John review the material; he turned in every assignment and his average for the second half of the semester improved to 49%. John also received the highest score in the class on his final exam, 72%. When the final scores were calculated, John's equaled 49.6%. Given Mr. Hartpence's grading scale, John missed passing the course with a "D" by .4 of a point.

Normally Mr. Hartpence would have passed John because he worked so hard and had significantly improved. This semester, however, Mr. Hartpence perceived a dilemma. Another student in his class, Ed, not a special education student, wound up with virtually the same score for the semester as John. Unlike John, Ed had done very little work in the class. Ed earned a "D" in the first half of the semester and, because he turned in only half of the total assignments, received a failing grade in the second half. Ed's final exam grade was low, but high enough for his average for the semester to equal John's.

Ms. Padilla was very concerned. If Mr. Hartpence were totally impartial and stuck to his original grading scale, he would have to fail both students and they would both have to repeat the course. This seemed unproblematic in Ed's case, given his overall lack of effort. However, if John failed the course, it could discourage him from ever working hard again because his best efforts would have failed. In turn, he might give up on trying to complete high school. Mr. Hartpence asked Ms. Padilla to help him make the decision.

What should Ms. Padilla advise Mr. Hartpence to do? Would it be fair to pass John and fail Ed?

DISCUSSION. The perceived dilemma in this case arises from the fact that John is in the regular biology class. Within this context, Mr. Hartpence (and apparently Ms. Padilla as well) believes that students such as Ed should be held accountable and failed if they don't measure up to the normal standards, whereas special allowances should be made to pass special education students. Because Ed's and John's scores are the same, they feel considerable pressure to either pass both or fail both, presumably in the name of fairness.

The easiest way out of the dilemma is to pass both ("easiest" in the sense that it would probably result in little or no outcry). In addition to being easy, this solution is also quite defensible, because both John and Ed are so close to passing and because failing the course would be quite harmful to both. This is the solution we would endorse, given the circumstances as they exist. On the other hand, there is one feature of this situation, namely, Mr. Hartpence's grading scheme, that merits closer scrutiny.

It is odd that John would pass were it not for Ed. This makes the grading scheme appear arbitrary, such that whether John passes or fails depends on which other students happen to be taking biology the same semester as he. If Mr. Hartpence believes that improvement and effort ought to be reflected in the grade (which seems implicit in his as well as Ms. Padilla's reasoning that John should pass and Ed should fail), then he should simply make that explicit. If he were to do so, then problems such as the one he faces regarding John and Ed would not arise. Furthermore, that John was a special education student would not even have to enter the picture, since it was his effort and improvement that led Mr. Hartpence and Ms. Padilla to think that he should probably pass.

Although we have made several suggestions regarding a resolution to this particular case, Mr. Hartpence's and Ms. Padilla's puzzlement is indicative of the more general issue of whether it is fair to regular students for special education students to be evaluated in terms of different, and presumably less demanding, standards. For instance, suppose John's average had been 45% or he had been given less demanding assignments. Should he then pass the same course that students like Ed would fail?

This question has no easy answer, and it goes to the heart of the practice of grading and the aims of special education. As things stand now, grades are typically used both to reward achievement and to predict how successful students might be later in their educational careers (consider their use in college admissions). Setting aside how grading and its uses might be criticized, if the aim of special education is to provide students with the extra help they need to be successful in and receive the benefits of the standard curriculum (and here Amy Rowley comes to mind, as well as John), then it seems appropriate to hold them responsible for the same performance as regular students. If, on the other hand, the aims are markedly different—for instance, providing "survival skills," fostering socialization, preparing special education students to live the richest life of which they are capable—then a different set of standards and responsibilities, which might be negotiated as part of an IEP, seems appropriate.

Unfortunately, this analysis leads to two further problems. First, it can lead to a "slippery slope" in which the standard curriculum and its associated expectations are seen as inappropriate for special education students in general. (We will examine this issue in the case that immediately follows.) Second, the problem remains of whether the same aims and standards should be adopted for integrated special education students as for regular education students. We grappled with various dimensions of this problem in Chapter 3, and we invite the reader to again ponder the issue.

Case: Teacher as Friend?

Rose Shur has been a special education teacher for 3 years. This is her first year at Spring Junior High School. She and Ray Wilson teach most of the classes for students in special education. Mr. Wilson, who has been at Spring for the past 8 years, has a very definite philosophy for working with adolescents. He considers this philosophy the basis for his teaching style. Because as a youngster he experienced severe adjustment problems and often felt frustrated and isolated, Mr. Wilson firmly believes that the root of all adolescents' problems is emotional. Although he has students with a variety of handicapping conditions, including learning disabilities, his major concern is to help students "feel good about themselves."

Mr. Wilson is genuinely interested in his students' problems, and they trust and confide in him. Part of helping the adolescents, according to Mr. Wilson, is being lenient and nonjudgmental, which to him means allowing frequent unexcused absences, exercising little follow-through on written assignments, avoiding much classroom structure and planning, and using class time to have friendly individual discussions about personal problems, movies, rock groups, and so forth.

In Mr. Wilson's class students are given reading and writing projects according to their abilities as judged by him; completion dates are left open, so much so that projects often are not completed at all. Students are allowed to bring other homework projects to class and in general to work on their own with little or no direction. Mr. Wilson requires no group projects and provides few guidelines for the infrequent assignments he does give. Mr. Wilson says, "You have to be their friend. If you're not, they won't come back." Often, because of Mr. Wilson's emphasis on individual work and giving personal attention to one student at a time, students in his class sleep, chatter and play, or even leave the classroom.

Mr. Wilson's teaching style is very disturbing to Ms. Shur. She believes it wastes time that ought to be used for teaching and learning. Furthermore, it adversely affects her own efforts: When she tries to work with students in a more active and directive way, they respond with questions like, "Why can't you be a friend like Mr. Wilson?" Although Ms. Shur is also concerned about students' problems, she believes this is not inconsistent with guiding them and holding them responsible for their assignments and behavior. In fact, she believes that not providing direction, structure, and guidelines amounts to shirking one's professional responsibility as a teacher and reflects a fundamental disrespect for students.

Is Mr. Wilson's teaching style appropriate for special education students? How far should special education teachers go in being their students' friend?

DISCUSSION. One can rightly question whether it is wise for Mr. Wilson to base his philosophy and teaching style on his personal experience as an adolescent. His failure to provide even the most minimal guidance, to require students to complete assignments, and to plan classroom activities looks like a rationalization for devoting very little effort to teaching under the guise of being "nonjudgmental" and a friend. Given the available evidence, Ms. Shur seems to have good support for her view that Mr. Wilson is simply shirking his professional responsibilities and that he displays a fundamental disrespect (a don't care attitude) toward his students' intellectual development. Mr. Wilson's approach also might be criticized for failing to take account of the long-term consequences for his students with respect to their subsequent education, and for fostering something akin to "learned helplessness" in his students vis-à-vis what they can and should be expected to accomplish in their formal education.

These criticisms of Mr. Wilson's purported teaching style do not imply that teachers, especially special education teachers, should not take a personal interest in their students and should not treat them with encouragement, compassion, understanding, and empathy. This is especially true regarding students with severe emotional problems. But insofar as their role is a professional one, teachers' relationship with students should stop somewhat short of friendship, both because children require prodding and guidance and because teachers in general (like doctors, psychologists, lawyers, and other professionals) should keep some carefully measured "distance" from those whom they serve. Such a distance helps them to maintain their own emotional well-being, to avoid overstepping the bounds of their authority, and to preserve a reasonable degree of impartiality among students.

What Ms. Shur should do about the situation as it exists involves the issue of professional relationships, which we examined in greater detail in the preceding chapter. Briefly, she should first approach Mr. Wilson with her concerns (at least initially withholding her assessment). Although it seems unlikely, he might change his approach or, which is perhaps more likely, he and Ms. Shur may be able to negotiate some sort of compromise. If this tack is unsuccessful, then Ms. Shur should pursue other avenues, for example, raising the issue with the principal, the special education supervisor, and so forth. There do not seem to be very good reasons to be optimistic, for apparently Mr. Wilson's teaching style was not questioned before Ms. Shur came to Spring. It thus seems that Mr. Wilson's approach enjoys the approval (at least tacitly) of his superiors.

CHAPTER 6

Conclusion: Professional Ethics and Compromise

In this chapter we provide a brief characterization of the ethical dimensions of negotiation and compromise. Although we have broached the issues of compromise in various of our case discussions, we have forestalled a systematic discussion of compromise until our concluding chapter for two primary reasons. First, such a discussion can probably best be appreciated only after grappling firsthand with a number of ethical issues in which the existence of divergent positions begs for negotiation and compromise. Second, the contemporary interest in the ethics of compromise is somewhat new and inchoate, and has been prompted largely by the increased interest in applied and professional ethics. Thus, it is fitting to end with the ethics of compromise because developing an adequate understanding of its nature and role within professional ethics is part and parcel of the continued development of the field of professional ethics itself.

In Chapter 1 we observed that the aim of ethical deliberation may be characterized as attempting to answer the question, "What, *all things considered*, ought to be done in a given situation?" (Benjamin & Curtis, 1986, p. 9); in Chapter 2 we observed that liberal democratic societies are based on the premise that individuals ought to have the freedom to adopt and the power to pursue their own view of the good life, constrained only by the requirement that their views and pursuits do not preclude others from enjoying the same freedom and power. Combining these two observations leads to the central importance of compromise, for one of the things that must be plugged into the *all things considered* clause is other people's views.

There are different ways of taking other people's views seriously, not all of which are ways of "compromising." Consider the following three examples. First, an individual might be convinced through argument that his or her initial view was mistaken and that it should be changed to agree with one offered by someone else. Second, an individual might change an initial view because he or she is the sort of person who seems to have no strongly held views of his or her own and readily adapts the "politically correct" view. Or, third, an individual might change an initial view because he or she is the sort of person who adopts whatever view best serves his or her self-interests once the handwriting is on the wall.

We do not believe the above three examples illustrate what it means to compromise. In the first example, on the basis of argument, one is led to adopt a different conclusion, to change one's mind about what is correct, and the need to compromise thus vanishes. The second two examples give "compromise" a bad name, for each involves a kind of "lack of principle." Moreover, like the first example, they, too, fail to illustrate true compromises, insofar as the individuals described simply changed their initial views.

In our view, a genuine moral compromise does not consist of changing one's mind. Rather, it consists of what Benjamin (1990) calls "splitting the difference" between one's own viewpoint and opposing viewpoints, while *at the same time* preserving one's integrity by remaining committed to one's original beliefs and principles. We will illustrate how this works by returning once again to the case of Amy Rowley and considering it in terms of some of the details of the view of moral compromise articulated by Benjamin.

According to Benjamin (1990), the existence of some or all of the following circumstances gives rise to the need to compromise: factual uncertainty, moral complexity, the need to maintain a continuing cooperative relationship, the need for a more or less immediate decision or action, and a scarcity of resources (p. 32). The first two circumstances, factual uncertainty and moral complexity, are sources of doubt that serve to reduce the degree of confidence that can attach to competing viewpoints on given ethical problems. This, in turn, provides an impetus and a justification for parties to a dispute to reach a middle ground. In the Rowley case whether providing Amy with an interpreter would indeed improve her performance was a source of factual uncertainty. How the concept of equal educational opportunity should be interpreted vis-à-vis the limit of schools' responsibility was a source of moral complexity.

The need to maintain a continuing cooperative relationship is a virtually ubiquitous circumstance that exists whenever individuals want to remain associated with a group. Different levels of association, of course, call for different degrees of cooperation, depending on both the intensity of interpersonal relationships (compare membership in a family with membership in a community) and the nature of authority structures (compare totalitarian and democratic regimes). Schools represent a relatively intimate level of association and, accordingly, their members must pay careful attention to maintaining cooperative relationships, both internally and in relation to external constituencies. In Amy Rowley's case, it would be desirable to maintain good relationships within the school, for example, between special and regular education, as well as with Amy's parents and other parents and organized groups that might support them.

The need to make more or less immediate decisions is also a frequent circumstance of schooling—children have to be placed, schedules have to be made, materials have to be ordered, teachers have to be assigned, and so forth. This circumstance often eliminates the luxury of time for sustained reflection. The clock was running on Amy Rowley's first-grade year, and a decision needed to be made regarding just how much would be provided for her by way of special services.

Finally, scarcity of resources is another frequently occurring circumstance of schooling. Considering the resources available, questions such as the following must be answered: How many new teachers can be hired? What is class size going to be? How many new books are going to be purchased? Should the band get new uniforms? Should the TAG program be expanded? What if the millage election fails? And, regarding Amy Rowley, what if the level of service her parents want must be provided to everyone?

In addition to enumerating the "circumstances of compromise," Benjamin also discusses what he calls "integrity preserving" compromise. Briefly, because individuals seek (or at least should seek) to preserve their personal identity, commitments, projects, and integrity, parties to a disagreement cannot be required to abandon their initial beliefs and principles in order to reach agreement. Rather, an appreciation of the "circumstances of compromise" motivates "splitting the difference" as the only way in which to resolve disagreements in a manner that shows respect for all concerned. Consider what kind of compromise might have been reached in the Rowley case to avoid having it wind up in court.

Amy's parents held that she should be provided with an interpreter in the classroom so that she would enjoy an opportunity to "maximize her potential commensurate with the opportunity provided to other children." The school authorities held that providing Amy with instruction in lip reading and with a hearing aid was sufficient because it permitted her to perform above average academically and to be socially well-adjusted. Viewed as a conflict between the principle of maximizing Amy's potential and the principle of providing her with sufficient help to ensure that she performs at an average level or above, the disagreement will remain at an impasse. However, the parties might be able to split the difference by accepting a middle ground that acknowledges the uncertainty involved, particularly regarding the factual question of how much an interpreter would help Amy.

Amy's parents and the school authorities disagreed regarding how much an interpreter would help Amy. Because both considered the issue relevant, however, testing it would be one way in which a compromise could be reached that "splits the difference," that gives something, but not everything, to each party to the disagreement. In particular, assume for the sake of argument that some resources were available to pay for an interpreter for Amy. Given this assumption, Amy's parents and the school authorities could compromise their extreme positions and agree to a trial period of, say, one semester in which Amy would be provided with an interpreter (many other variations can be imagined). If she improved significantly, then every effort would be made to continue providing the interpreter; if she did not, then the school would cease providing the interpreter.

Notice this compromise does not turn on settling the "matter of principle," but instead turns on removing factual uncertainty. Although the school authorities believed that enabling Amy to perform above average was all that could be reasonably demanded of them, they might very well be moved to change their position vis-à-vis the need for an interpreter if providing Amy with an interpreter enabled her to perform significantly better. Although Amy's parents believed that it was the school's responsibility to maximize Amy's potential, they might very well be moved to change their position if providing Amy with an interpreter made only a negligible difference in her performance.

Complicating the general picture sketched so far in terms of the Rowley case, compromise takes on added dimensions for professionals because of their role-related obligations. We will illustrate how by briefly re-examining three cases discussed in previous chapters, focusing, in turn, on compromise and integrity, compromise and working relationships, and compromise and personal characteristics.

The case entitled, Parents' Wishes Versus Professional Judgment (p. 83) illustrates integrity preserving compromise in light of professional commitments, both when compromise is and is not possible. We suggested in our discussion that a compromise was in order between Ms. Burns (the special education teacher) and Ms. James about whether Ms. James' daughter Rosie, a kindergartner with severe intellectual difficulties, should be integrated into the regular classroom for a portion of the school day. We suggested, in particular, that a strategy along the lines of the one suggested above in the Rowley case, in which Ms. James would agree to a trial period to see how Rosie fared with integration, should be tried. This would be an integrity preserving compromise for both Ms. Burns and Ms. James. We went on to suggest, however, that if Ms. James wouldn't agree, then Ms. Burns would have to walk away from the situation and suggest to Ms. James that she seek another placement for Rosie. Here we were suggesting that, were Ms. James to remain unconvinced, an integrity-preserving compromise—one that would permit Ms. Burns to remain faithful to her deeply held conviction about integration and her associated role-related obligations—was not possible.

Another case, Power Grab in the Staffing (p. 29), illustrates how working relationships form part of the background conditions that determine whether compromise is possible. Recall that Dr. Anderson, the school psychologist, ran roughshod over the staffing for a fifth grader, Mary Brown, although there was considerable factual uncertainty about whether she should be placed in special education at all. Dr. Anderson's refusal to take seriously the views of others, combined with the inability or unwillingness of other members of the staffing team to press for a more collaborative and democratic process, guaranteed that there would be no "splitting the difference" regarding what to do about Mary. This case thus illustrates the inherently democratic nature of compromise. Within the professional context, individuals must be accorded equal respect and authority sufficient to enable them to meaningfully express their views and to ensure that their views have a chance of influencing the outcome of deliberations and negotiations. Consistent with this, professional expertise must be kept within its proper bounds and not allowed (as it was allowed in the case of Dr. Anderson) to overwhelm other legitimate interests and perspectives.

Finally, the case, Resistance to Integration (p. 66) illustrates the personal dimension of compromise. In this case we could not agree on whether Ms. Rollins, a resource room teacher, should accept a "deal" (i.e., a compromise) regarding integrating her students into the regular classroom. In the face of school-wide resistance to integration by experienced teachers, Mr. Jones, the principal of the school, had cajoled (perhaps coerced) Mr. Young, a new teacher, into cooperating with Ms. Rollins. However, the form that the integration was to take was a far cry from true integration, and Ms. Rollins was put in the position of deciding whether to accept it, in the hope that it might lead to something better rather than something worse.

In our discussion, we did not disagree about the facts but about whether the risks involved were worth taking. (Miramontes thought they were; Howe thought they were not.) It could be simply that one of us has incorrectly estimated the risks or is otherwise mistaken. But there is an alternative explanation: We could be implicitly filling in missing information about Ms. Rollins's characteristics in different ways. For example, perhaps Howe assumed she is less patient and less able to lead people in directions they may not want to go than Miramontes did. This would help explain why Howe would think a compromise was a bad idea and why Miramontes would disagree. Whatever the source of our disagreement, the general point we wish to make is that who an individual is can be relevant to the advisability of agreeing to a given compromise, particularly from the point of view of the individuals directly involved. For example, it would make more sense for Ms. Rollins to agree to the compromise if she were secure, respected, and socially adept within the school than if she were not. This does not imply some vicious sort of moral relativism. Rather, in keeping with Socrates's advice to "know thyself," it acknowledges that knowing one's strengths and weaknesses and incorporating them into decisions about what actions to undertake is a wise thing to do, in light of the consequences for both others and oneself.

In the end, there is, of course, no guarantee that compromises can always (or even usually) get off the ground (one or both of the parties might be intransigent, no extra resources might be available, and so forth). Further, there is no assurance that compromises will not fail at some time later, even when they do initially get off the ground (one of the parties might renege, disagreement might surface after initial agreement, and so forth). However, this is no reason not to pursue compromise whenever it looks promising. At the individual level, engaging in compromise is a way to get at least part of what one thinks is right, without its being a threat to integrity. When parties to a dispute make a good faith effort to reach a compromise solution, they need not abandon their interests, principles, and commitments; instead, they need only exercise a certain degree of humility and show due respect for the interests, principles, and commitments of others. At the institutional level, working relationships that facilitate compromise are much more conducive to mutual respect and cohesive school relationships than is blind adherence to rules and laws or, which often comes to the same thing, sheer appeal to power and position. In this connection, even when attempts to compromise fail to yield satisfactory *outcomes*, the *process* of engaging in them reinforces important norms.

This brief account of the nature and value of compromise completes the project of this book. We have endeavored to both identify the general nature of the ethics of special education and suggest how particular issues and situations might be best approached. Naturally, we would be pleased if readers find themselves largely agreeing with us. On the other hand, if we have only managed to help map the terrain and to provide some useful tools for navigating it, our project will have been a success.

APPENDIX A

Cases for Discussion

This appendix contains 12 cases that are of the same general form as those we have discussed so far throughout the book. We offer them as grist for further discussion, as paper topics, or for whatever creative uses they might be put to by instructors and students. Although we hope that the preceding discussions and categories prove relevant and helpful, we have decided against topically arranging the cases because real-world problems don't come labeled as problems in the distribution of educational resources, problems in professional relationships, and so forth. And, as has been demonstrated in the discussion of previous cases, how individuals view a particular situation can shift depending on their relationship to it. Finally, we urge instructors and students to go beyond the cases we provide and to develop their own upon which to collaboratively reflect. There often simply is no substitute for the details and nuances that can be supplied by someone who has actually lived through a perplexing ethical problem.

Case 1: Reward for a Job Well Done?

Ms. Teel has been a resource teacher at Silver Elementary School for 4 years. The community is small and many parents know each other. The other special education teacher at Silver is Ms. Rusk. Although the two teachers have adjacent resource rooms, their styles are quite different. Ms. Rusk is very traditional and feels that repetition and drill are important for developing skills, particularly in students with learning disabilities. Parents find her difficult to talk with and come away feeling Ms. Rusk believes that if *they* just worked together with their children, their children would succeed. Ms. Teel, on the other hand, is open, well-organized, and flexible, and has excellent rapport with her students. Parents like her child-centered attitude, and she is very supportive of them.

Not surprisingly, Ms. Teel has become the "favorite" special education teacher at Silver. Many parents have requested that she work with their children, and her student load has grown to 25 (Ms. Rusk's is 19). Because of her heavy load, Ms. Teel is concerned that the level of service she provides to children is being diminished. Consequently, she approached the principal and received assurances that he would do all he could to avoid further increasing her case load.

A few days later, Ms. Johnson, a parent whom Ms. Teel knows well, stopped her in the hall and told her that the pressure in Ms. Rusk's class was too much for her son Mark, and was emphatic about making a change for him. She asked Ms. Teel if Mark could go to her instead of Ms. Rusk for his resource room help. Ms. Teel explained that it was not her decision and that Ms. Johnson would have to take it up with the principal.

The next day the principal asked Ms. Teel to meet with him. He asked her if it would be possible to accommodate Mark in her resource room schedule. He told her that both he and Ms. Johnson felt that Mark would be much better off in her room because he so greatly needed her flexible and open style. He said this was just a request and that Mark would not be moved without her consent.

Ms. Teel also felt sure that Mark would benefit from working with her, but that taking him would further compromise her ability to work with her other students. She was also distressed that the principal did not help alleviate this situation for her. She wondered whether these requests would ever end and about the fairness of her case load versus Ms. Rusk's.

- Should the principal do more to insulate Ms. Teel from parental demands?
- Is the situation fair to Ms. Teel? To the students in Ms. Rusk's class?
- What should Ms. Teel do?

Case 2: Arbitrary and Capricious Placement Criteria?

Mr. Glenn is the principal at Commons Elementary School, an inner-city school in a low-income community. He received a call one day from Robert Cunningham concerning the transfer of Mr. Cunningham's son Martin, a fifth grader, to Commons. Mr. Cunningham told Mr. Glenn that Martin had been receiving special education services for learning disabilities for the past 3 years, and that he wanted to apprise Mr. Glenn of this to make sure that the services wouldn't be interrupted. Specifically, Martin had been receiving an hour a day of intensive assistance in reading and math in the resource room.

Mr. Glenn reassured Mr. Cunningham that Martin would receive the same special education services at Commons that he had in his former school. Mr. Glenn pointed out, however, that as a matter of "routine" Martin's school records would have to be reviewed and a full assessment would have to be conducted at Commons. Mr. Cunningham was satisfied with Mr. Glenn's reassurances, but requested feedback on the outcome of the process as soon as it was available.

Within the week Commons received Martin's records from his previous school (which was located in an affluent community in another state). The records revealed that Martin had originally been placed in special education for emotional/behavioral disturbances and that he had made good progress and had adjusted well to the school setting. The records also revealed that his IEPs had changed over time, moving from a focus on affective needs to a focus on academic needs, and that he had been recategorized as learning disabled. Based on the assessment at Commons, however, Martin did not meet the district's criteria for learning disabilities. Thus, Martin failed to qualify for special education services at Commons, and Mr. Glenn took steps to have him removed from special education.

When Mr. Glenn called Mr. Cunningham to give him the (good?) news, Mr. Cunningham was surprised and angered. He said it was absurd that Martin could have learning disabilities in one state and miraculously lose them by crossing the border. He accused Mr. Glenn of being arbitrary and capricious, and, slamming down the phone, said that this wasn't the end of the matter and that Mr. Glenn could expect to hear from the superintendent.

- What are the sources of this problem?
- What should Mr. Glenn do?

Case 3: Double Jeopardy

Mr. Fleet, a fourth-grade teacher, supports the concept of integration because he believes that everyone should have the same opportunities for learning. Several students spend approximately 3 hours a day in the resource room and the rest of their day in Mr. Fleet's room. Because their resource room schedules vary, they leave Mr. Fleet's classroom at various times throughout the day, often during instructional activities.

Mr. Fleet requires all the students in his class to do the same amount of work and grades all students on the basis of the same criteria. This approach creates certain problems for the special education students:

They have more homework because they miss out on time provided for work in the classroom, they often lack understanding because they miss instruction, and they are frequently admonished because they often do not have their work completed.

Eventually, Mr. Fleet assigned an aide specifically to the task of providing extra help for these students. They had fallen so far behind, however, that it looked as if they would never catch up. Mr. Fleet believed that he and the resource room teacher had worked things out the best they could, and remained firm in his belief that these students should have to do the same amount of work and measure up to the same standards as his other students. Giving them less work or relaxing the standards would be coddling them, unfair to the other students, and counter to the whole point of mainstreaming. Despite himself and what he thought was right, Mr. Fleet began to perceive these students as just lazy and unmotivated, and began to have serious doubts about the feasibility of integration.

- What is fair in this case, and to whom?
- Do better alternatives exist?
- Is Mr. Fleet's commitment to integration too shallow?

Case 4: Medication or Else

Bobby Hanes is a fourth grader who has been in special education for over a year for an emotional disturbance. Bobby is aggressive and always on the move, constantly fidgeting, getting out of his seat and interrupting and disturbing other children in the class. Bobby currently spends 4 hours a day in the resource room and 2 hours in the regular classroom.

Bobby is not making very good progress. Although he is able to exert limited control when other groups in the resource room are small, he often loses control during the several times a day when the resource room is full. Because he has even more difficulty following the rules in his regular classroom and is becoming increasingly aggressive, Mr. Erickson, Bobby's regular classroom teacher, has suggested that Bobby should be in a more restrictive and structured setting for the entire school day.

Mr. Kay, the resource specialist, feels strongly that if Bobby's behavior could be brought under control, it would allow him to remain in a less restrictive setting, which, in Mr. Kay's judgment, is vital to Bobby's preadolescent development. Mr. Kay's experience leads him to believe that Bobby is a good candidate for medication (e.g., ritalin) to control his hyperactivity and that he should see a physician with this in mind.

Mr. Kay decided to broach the subject with Bobby's mother, Janet Hanes, who had always been a helpful and concerned parent. He was very surprised by her violent reaction to the idea. She told him that under no circumstances would she permit her son to be placed on medication and that she resented Mr. Kay for wanting to "drug" her child. She blamed drugs for the breakup of her marriage and would not allow her son to be involved in drug treatment of any kind.

Mr. Kay reminded Ms. Hanes that the yearly review of Bobby's progress was coming up the following month and told her that if Bobby's disruptive behavior continued, he feared the staffing committee would see placing Bobby in a self-contained classroom for emotional disturbances as their only alternative. He pointed out that this would limit Bobby's interaction with other students and probably exacerbate his problems. He also pointed out that such a change in placement would require moving Bobby to another school located a considerable distance from his home. Mr. Kay urged Ms. Hanes to reconsider her position.

- Does Mr. Kay want to "drug" Bobby as an easy way out?
- Did Mr. Kay approach this situation in the best way?
- What if Ms. Hanes remains steadfast?

Case 5: Do the Ends Justify the Means?

Bill Hunt, a resource room teacher at Washington Junior High School, is particularly frustrated with Dale Jenkins, one of his eighth-grade students. Dale has a learning disability associated with difficulty in math. (Dale has not passed a single semester's math class since he entered junior high school.) Mr. Hunt is convinced, however, that Dale could do much better if he would just apply himself.

Mr. Hunt observed that during instruction Dale frequently just stares passively at the teacher or at other students, rarely listening or volunteering to answer questions. He often just draws pictures. Other teachers report similar behaviors in their classrooms.

Dale typically comes to the resource room with a group of six other students. Because Dale is popular with this group, Mr. Hunt decided to try to use peer pressure to get Dale to work. Mr. Hunt soon was again frustrated because neither praising the other students nor holding them up as positive role models had any effect on Dale. Mr. Hunt then decided to take drastic measures. Whenever he saw Dale drawing pictures he collected them and showed them to the rest of the group in an attempt to embarrass and ridicule Dale. Somewhat to Mr. Hunt's surprise, this last-ditch effort seemed to be working. Dale stopped drawing pictures and began attempting some of the problems during class. By the end of the term Dale's work in the resource room had improved tremendously and he had earned a "C" in his math class as well.

- Was Mr. Hunt right to use this tactic to reach Dale?
- What other alternatives might he have tried?
- Could there be any undesirable effects resulting from this tactic?

Case 6: Teaching Responsibility or Limiting Opportunity?

Anita is a quiet and reserved fifth grader with a severe hearing impairment. She wears a hearing aid, which helps her function effectively in school. However, Anita often forgets to bring the batteries for the hearing aid to school with her. To remedy this problem, Ms. Long asked Anita and her parents to supply an extra battery that could be kept in Anita's desk, and her parents responded by sending three batteries to school with Anita. This worked temporarily, but no more batteries were provided after the three were expended. Calls to Anita's home revealed that Anita had new batteries, but neglected to bring them to school. As a consequence, Anita had again been without the use of her hearing aid on several occasions.

Ms. Long believed that she had been very patient, but had now become quite irritated with Anita. Coping with Anita when she couldn't hear disrupted the class routine and made working with her very difficult. Ms. Long felt Anita was being very irresponsible and that it was a good time for her to learn a sense of responsibility. After all, someone was not always going to be there to take care of her, so she needed to learn to take care of herself. Ms. Long decided that from then on, whenever Anita forgot her batteries she could just sit in class all day without them, receiving no special attention.

- Will this action help Anita learn to be more responsible?
- What if it doesn't?
- Was Ms. Long's decision too hasty?

Case 7: EBD—A Label for Protection?

At the end of every school year the counselors, principals, and staff members at Hawthorne Junior High School meet to discuss the possible retention of seventh-, eighth-, and ninth-grade students who have failed two or more classes prior to the fourth quarter. This process is used to determine whether students have a chance of being promoted to the next higher grade level provided they pass all their remaining classes and/or attend summer school.

Tom, a seventh grader, presented the committee with a particularly difficult situation. During the fourth quarter Tom was identified as having an emotional/behavioral disorder (EBD) and placed in a self-contained classroom for half the day. Prior to Tom's staffing he had been involved in more than 14 fights, numerous incidents in which he cursed faculty members, student harassment and intimidation, and smoking marijuana in a classroom. Needless to say, Tom was in very serious trouble prior to being placed in the self-contained setting. He was failing all his classes and had he gotten into trouble just one more time, he would automatically have been expelled.

Following his special education placement 6 weeks previously, Tom had made good improvement in his behavior in classrooms, including passing five of his courses during the fourth quarter (though he continued to swear at, shove, and generally harass other students between classes). Tom had accumulated a total of five credits and, according to normal criteria, needed nine to be promoted to the eighth grade.

The two special education teachers were very pleased with Tom's improvement and strongly supported promoting him. They believed that retaining him could only have detrimental effects (one of them also believed that retention is *in general* harmful). They also pointed to the fact that Tom's parents had recently gone through a protracted and nasty divorce that had been quite stressful for Tom. In addition, his mother, with whom he now lived, could not afford tuition for summer school. Finally, they pointed out that Tom had been a "B+" student until seventh grade and that he had recently begun pulling himself back up.

The remainder of the committee disagreed with the special education teachers' recommendation, believing that four credits were too many to waive. They also believed that promoting Tom would simply "reward" him for his misbehavior and that he should be required to face the consequences that he had created for himself, like any other "regular" student. They felt the fact that Tom had previously been a "B+" student supported just the opposite of what the special education teachers thought: namely, that Tom should know better and that if he applied himself, he could easily get back on track and catch up on the content he had failed to learn.

- Should Tom be promoted?
- Should the fact that he has an emotional/behavioral disorder make a difference?

Case 8: Who Decides the Curriculum?

Ms. Kline is the special education teacher at Fairview Elementary School. Except for a reading specialist, she is the only teacher trained and certified to work with special needs students.

Approximately 10 years previously she created the learning lab (LL) at Fairview to meet students' learning needs, independent of whether they qualified for special education. The LL was staffed by volunteer parents and high school students who were enrolled in preteaching classes at the local high school. Ms. Kline kept a watchful eye on the LL. She was very proud of her creation and believed it met the needs of many students who otherwise would have great difficulty in school.

Classroom teachers referred students to the LL, and students were admitted only with parental consent. The general form of the LL program was two 30-minute pull-out periods a week. In order to make training volunteers and giving them teaching responsibilities feasible, each child assigned to the LL was prescribed a program with predetermined materials and teaching methods. The program emphasized building self-esteem and providing one-on-one interactions. It also emphasized returning children totally to the regular classroom program when they no longer required extra support. Thus, at the end of each year all students were evaluated to determine whether they should remain in the LL the following year.

Johnny is a second grader who is just finishing his first year in the LL program. He was placed in the LL because of his exceptionally low achievement in math and because he was overly shy and standoffish. Based on the results of his end-of-year assessment, Ms. Kline judged that he could still benefit from the LL and recommended that he continue in it for at least one more year.

Ms. Grove, Johnny's third-grade teacher-to-be (who was widely recognized as an effective and devoted teacher) was opposed. In her view, the work her students did in the LL needed to tie directly to their classroom activities, and in her experience such coordination rarely (if ever) occurred between classrooms and the LL. Thus, she would not agree to having Johnny attend the LL unless she could specify what academic work he would be doing there. She felt that if Johnny was going to be pulled out of her class, he shouldn't waste precious time just "playing games with a buddy from the high school." Indeed, she felt so strongly about it that she said she would call Johnny's parents and tell them her opinion.

Ms. Kline felt that Ms. Grove was too "content oriented" and that she failed to appreciate Johnny's need for the positive social interactions that occurred between himself and his so-called "buddy" in order to develop communication skills and greater self-confidence. In terms of her own expertise, and as a practical matter, she thought it was inappropriate and unreasonable to demand that the LL program accommodate individual teacher requests with regard to what students should work on. She contemplated arranging a staffing to determine whether Johnny fit the criteria for learning disabilities, with an eye toward including participation in the LL in his IEP.

- Should Ms. Kline proceed with such a plan?
- Does Ms. Grove have a legitimate complaint?
- What kind of compromise might be reached?

Case 9: Who Should Pay?

Mike Williams is a second grader at Wilson Elementary School. He lives with his mother, Dorothy Andrews, and two older siblings in government-subsidized, low-income housing. Ms. Andrews changes jobs frequently and receives state assistance.

Mike is a troubled boy. As a young child he was abused by his father; he has been in trouble several times with the fire department for starting fires; his behavior at home is generally very disruptive; and he is often depressed and withdrawn, and has talked about killing himself.

Not surprisingly, Mike also has great difficulty in school. He was staffed into a self-contained classroom for emotional disturbances the previous year at his former school. He entered Wilson after having spent several months in the children's hospital, where ritalin was prescribed three times a day. Mike was still taking ritalin when he entered Wilson, and he was staffed into the resource room for 3 hours a day, again for emotional disturbances. In addition to his other problems, Mike exhibited low academic skills.

In the resource room at Wilson, Mike's teacher, Eric Benn, employed behavior modification techniques in an attempt to eliminate Mike's antisocial behavior and to improve his academic skills. Over several months, Mike's behavior became more manageable and he began to master some basic academic skills. Mike was starting to find success in school and even seemed to be starting to enjoy his classes.

Eventually, however, Mike regressed. He again became frustrated with his assignments, experienced trouble concentrating, and began refusing to do his work. On several occasions he ripped up his assignments and threw them on the floor. Concerned and disappointed, Mr. Benn called Ms. Andrews to see if she might have some clue as to what was going on with Mike. After a somewhat lengthy pause, she confessed that she hadn't been able to afford the cost of Mike's ritalin and didn't know when (if ever) she would be able to buy it. She said that Medicaid had always paid for all her family's prescriptions and that she had recently been "cut off."

Mike's untoward behavior continued to escalate in the resource room, the halls, the lunchroom, his regular classroom, and on the playground. Mr. Benn again called Mike's mother and apprised her of the seriousness of the situation. She insisted that there was nothing she could do. She simply couldn't afford to pay for Mike's ritalin.

- Is Ms. Andrews guilty of medical neglect?
- Is Mike's inability to obtain ritalin the school's problem?
- What else might Mr. Benn do?

Case 10: No Label, No Service

Karl Schmidt is an eighth grader who has been at Grace Middle School for the past year. Karl is a very poor reader. He has few word attack skills, a limited vocabulary, and low comprehension.

The principal, the special education teacher, and several of Karl's other teachers advocated staffing Karl for a learning disability. Tim Nichols, Karl's language arts and social studies teacher, in whose classroom Karl spends half the day, was opposed. Mr. Nichols was somewhat skeptical of special education and how it, in his eyes, "medicalized" all sorts of "ordinary problems in living and learning," particularly with respect to "mild needs" such as learning disabilities. He thought special education should be the last resort, rather than the first.

Mr. Nichols had taken it upon himself to look into Karl's background and found that Karl's family, participating in Karl's father's rise up the corporate ladder, had only recently settled down after moving around a great deal over the previous several years. Mr. Nichols thought that Karl's frequent moves provided a clear, "commonsense" explanation of his reading difficulties that was superior to the explanation that he must have a learning disability.

Karl's academic progress has been somewhat slow in his year-and-a-half at Grace, and Mr. Nichols recognized that Karl did indeed have special academic needs. But he thought it was ridiculous to have to label Karl as learning disabled in order to provide him with extra help. He also thought that the staffing process would be very hard on both Karl and his family and that Karl needed to be in the regular classroom in order to make friends and to fit into the community.

As an alternative to staffing Karl, Mr. Nichols volunteered to work with Karl individually, meeting with him before and after school if necessary. Not a total skeptic with regard to special education, Mr. Nichols expressed a willingness to take seriously any recommendations that Anne Hollingsworth, the special education teacher, might provide. In this connection, Mr. Nichols proposed that Ms. Hollingsworth conduct an "informal" evaluation on Karl and that she come to his classroom on a regular basis in order to help develop the materials Karl needed and to demonstrate the teaching methods that would be the best for Mr. Nichols to adopt.

Formal special education guidelines restricted Ms. Hollingsworth's role and responsibilities to working with students who had been explicitly placed into special education through the formal staffing process. Ms. Hollingsworth feared that if she agreed to Mr. Nichols' plan, other teachers would ask for the same type of assistance and that she would soon be overwhelmed. In addition, not only would she be stepping outside of the formal special education guidelines, but she would be taking time away from the students who had been placed into her special education classroom through the full staffing process. She was sympathetic to, and saw the merits of, Mr. Nichols' proposal (although she had to admit that in her heart of hearts she resented Mr. Nichols' general attitude about special education). All things considered, however, she could not accept Mr. Nichols' plan.

- Is Mr. Nichols' approach in general feasible?
- What do you think of his attitude toward special education?
- Did Ms. Hollingsworth make the right decision?

Case 11: What Does a High School Diploma Mean?

Fred Simmons is a senior at Jefferson High School and has been in special education classes since sixth grade. Fred always had severe difficulties with reading. On the other hand, he developed a number of alternative strategies to compensate for his reading difficulties; proved himself to be a good thinker, especially in math; and was generally perceived as likeable, responsible, and mature.

With the avowed goals of raising standards and ensuring the basic literacy and math competency of graduates, the state in which Jefferson is located instituted a uniform competency examination to be given to all high school seniors the year Fred was to graduate. Passing the examination became a condition of receiving a high school diploma. Students and their parents were advised 3 years previously when the new policy would take effect.

Fred had taken the test twice and, not surprisingly, had failed the reading portion each time. Mr. Sax, Fred's resource room teacher, had opposed the new policy from the start because of the negative consequences he foresaw for his students. A cursory look through the employment section of the local newspaper indicated that even the most unskilled kinds of jobs required a high school diploma. Mr. Sax was sure that Fred would make an excellent employee, especially if he could put his mathematics ability to good use. Without a diploma, however, it looked as though Fred wouldn't even be given the chance to prove himself.

Fred was very discouraged and complained to Mr. Sax that he had been "lied to" (not saying but intimating that Mr. Sax was the liar) and that all his years of struggling in school had been nothing but a waste of time. He also told Mr. Sax that he had told Steve, a tenth-grade friend of his who was also in special education, that he might as well drop out because he'd never be able to pass the "stupid test."

Mr. Sax felt terrible after this exchange, and he wondered if he really wasn't lying to his students (and himself). Not harboring any real hope, he nonetheless approached the principal, Mr. Bigelow, about finding an alternative method of showing what Fred could do. Mr. Bigelow was one of the new principals in the district in the vanguard of the higher standards movement (so much so that he supported the idea that schools should provide a "warranty" that their graduates exhibit a certain level of "quality"), and his response was wholly predictable. He said, "Reading is a basic requirement. If Fred can't read, I certainly can't, nor should I, go along with graduating him."

- Is the state policy justified?
- Should special allowances be made for special education students?
- What should Mr. Sax do?

Case 12: Treating Like Cases Alike?

Rich Wilson and Tim Evans are friends. Both are eighth graders at Stewart Junior High School, and both are having a very difficult time in school. They are often belligerent in class, have been involved in several fights after school, and are presently on suspension for wrestling a teacher to the floor who was attempting to stop a quarrel between Rich and another boy in the hall. Although both previously had been average students, their grades plummeted in the eighth grade. Because they were frequently absent and had a difficult time keeping up with their work, they became sullen, highly frustrated with schoolwork, and aggressive toward other students. As a result, both boys were referred for special education staffing. Testing revealed a discrepancy between achievement and aptitude for both Rich and Tim, though it was not as great as was usually associated with learning disabilities. Thus, both boys were being staffed for emotional disturbances.

Rich and Tim come from quite different social circumstances. Rich lives in an upper middle class neighborhood with both his parents. Mr. Wilson, Rich's father, is a successful businessman, an active member of several influential civic groups, and is generally well liked and respected in the community. Ms. Wilson, Rich's mother, is a certified elementary teacher who resigned her teaching position after 5 years to stay home to care for and raise her children (Rich has a 5-year-old sister). In contrast to Rich, Tim lives with his mother, Ms. Evans, in low-income housing. Ms. Evans has been divorced since Tim was 3 years old, and Tim's father hasn't been heard from in more than 5 years. In order to make ends meet, Ms. Evans works two unskilled jobs.

Rich's staffing occurred on Monday, November 11. As the discussion proceeded, Ms. Wilson became very upset about the fact that Rich was being considered for services for an emotional disturbance. She acknowledged that Rich has problems but insisted that a label of emotionally disturbed was unwarranted and would imply that Rich is mentally unstable (which, in turn, would reflect on his home life and parents). Given her teaching experience, she was well aware of the stigmatizing effect of identifying a child as emotionally disturbed. She proclaimed that she would agree to special education services for Rich, but only if they were provided under the rubric of a learning disability. Otherwise, she would not sign the IEP and would seek legal assistance.

With the exception of Ms. May, the resource room teacher, the staffing team believed that Rich should be identified as emotionally disturbed. Ms. May was sympathetic to Ms. Wilson's concerns about the effects of labeling Rich emotionally disturbed. She also supported Ms. Wilson's position on the grounds that Ms. Wilson was a former teacher, now spending her time raising her children, and could provide significant help for Rich at home. In the end, the team capitulated to Ms. Wilson and Ms. May, and agreed to classify Rich as learning disabled.

Tim's staffing occurred on Thursday, November 14, 3 days after Rich's. As the meeting proceeded, it became clear that Ms. Evans would be considerably less assertive than Ms. Wilson. She said that she had little experience with schools and that although she had quit school at 16, she now saw the value of education and had high hopes for Tim. She said that she tried to help Tim with his schoolwork whenever she had the time and energy, especially after she noticed his recent frustrations. She wished that she could spend more time with Tim, because he seemed to do much better on his schoolwork when she was able to sit and help him individually. She believed Tim had some sort of "block," as she put it.

The information presented at Tim's staffing was very similar to the information presented at Rich's. (Indeed, Rich and Tim had been involved in many of the same incidents.) Again, except for Ms. May, who, like Tim's mother, had also noticed some basic learning difficulties, the staffing team believed that a categorization of emotional disturbance was indicated. One of the claimed advantages of this category as compared with learning disabilities was that Tim would receive behavioral therapy (a benefit for him) and spend a greater percentage of time in the resource room, segregated from the rest of the students, particularly Rich (a benefit for everyone else). This time, unlike in the case of Rich, no protest was lodged by the parent. Ms. Evans said that the members of the team were the experts, that she felt sure they would be fair and do the best for her son, and that she would accept whatever they recommended.

As the meeting wound down, Mr. Hollyfield, the principal, who was sitting next to Ms. May, leaned over and whispered, "You won the last one. You're going to have to give this one to us."

- Should Ms. May go along with characterizing Tim as emotionally disturbed?
- Is Ms. Evans' trust in the integrity of the team and the process well founded?

APPENDIX B

Council for Exceptional Children (CEC) Code of Ethics

We declare the following principles to be the Code of Ethics for educators of exceptional persons. Members of the special education profession are responsible for upholding and advancing these principles. Members of The Council for Exceptional Children agree to judge by them in accordance with the spirit and provisions of this code.

I. Special education professionals are committed to developing the highest educational and quality of life potential of exceptional individuals.

II. Special education professionals promote and maintain a high level of competence and integrity in practicing their profession.

III. Special education professionals engage in professional activities which benefit exceptional individuals, their families, other colleagues, students, or research subjects.

IV. Special education professionals exercise objective professional judgment in the practice of their profession.

V. Special education professionals strive to advance their knowledge and skills regarding the education of exceptional individuals.

VI. Special education professionals work within the standards and policies of their profession.

VII. Special education professionals seek to uphold and improve where necessary the laws, regulations, and policies governing the deliv-

---

Reprinted from *Exceptional Children*, 50(3), 205, with the permission of the Council for Exceptional Children.

ery of special education and related services and the practice of their profession.

VIII. Special education professionals do not condone or participate in unethical or illegal acts, nor violate professional standards adopted by the Delegate Assembly of CEC.

APPENDIX C

Professional Ethical Codes and Ethical Deliberation

Professional ethical codes provide a somewhat more "neutral" approach to ethical issues than does religion (the topic of Appendix D), and it is customary among the professions to develop them. With the advent of the field of practical ("applied") ethics it has become just as customary for moral philosophers to point out the limited value of such codes in addressing particular ethical problems. We will begin with this limitation of ethical codes for teaching. Later, we will consider their positive value.

In general, a professional code of ethics seeks to articulate the creed of a given group of professionals. Such a group typically includes a great diversity of individuals with varying viewpoints on controversial issues, however, and thus, in order to win assent, the principles articulated in professional ethical codes must be exceedingly general—some would say they are merely platitudes. The resulting problem is that where principles are so general that they are virtually universally endorsed by a given group of professionals, they provide little by way of guidance regarding what to do in specific cases of ethical controversy.

As an illustration, consider the Rowley case (described in Chapters 1 and 2) in light of paragraph I of the CEC code. The code requires a commitment to "developing the highest educational and quality of life potential of exceptional individuals." But what shape should such a commitment take? Should special educators devote time after the normal school day to help students like Amy? Should they organize protest marches? Should they organize a strike? Should they testify in court? These questions, which are genuine and which we don't wish to dismiss, are simply not answered by the CEC code. To take another example, what does "highest" mean in the context of the code? Presumably, it means "highest possible," "highest reasonable," or something of that sort. But what is possible or reasonable under the factual conditions that existed vis-à-vis the constraints of P.L. 94–142 is exactly what is at issue regarding the services the schools should be required to provide children like Amy Rowley. Again, the CEC code seems too general to be of much help.

In addition to being too general, ethical codes are also limited insofar as the principles they enumerate may conflict. Consider a situation in which in order to obtain special education services deemed beneficial to a student, it is necessary to "stretch" or "finesse" the rules so that the student may qualify (see the case, Special Education: Opportunity or Stigma?, p. 70). Paragraphs I and III of the code seem to count in favor of providing services to such a student, whereas by virtue of their reference to the law, paragraphs VII and VIII count against it. The point is that the code is silent regarding what to do about conflicts among its principles. Thus, in order to decide which principle(s) should win out, it is necessary to get beyond the code. (Someone might object that the code is not relevant to this situation because the code applies to exceptional individuals only, and whether the child in question should be classified as exceptional is precisely what is at issue. Perhaps this is correct, but the general conclusion still holds: The code does not provide a means of deciding what to do.)

Ethical codes, then, will not make the need to engage in case-by-case ethical deliberation go away, but this is not to suggest they have no value. Ethical codes require professionals to give due consideration to the special duties and dangers that are inherent in their practice. Whereas physicians worry about things like unnecessary medical procedures for financial gain, nurses worry about things like protecting patients' interests without usurping physicians' authority, and journalists worry about purveying false and damaging stories, special educators worry about things like the possible harm that may result from labeling. The value to a profession of the initial process of clarifying ethical worries and codifying them in a set of principles is that it enhances ethical awareness; the ongoing value of an ethical code to a profession is that it continues to serve as a general guidepost and reminder of the ethical duties and dangers peculiar to the profession.

APPENDIX D

Religion and Ethical Deliberation

Many individuals turn to their religious beliefs when confronted with ethical problems, and religion is clearly a very important source of ethical guidance. On the other hand, the role of religious belief in ethical deliberation is limited, both because of the nature of the relationship between religion and ethics itself and because the deliberation in question must be consistent with a religiously pluralistic society.

Since Plato's Euthyphro many philosophers have argued that ethics must be autonomous—based on human judgment about what is right and wrong—rather than heteronomous—based on divine commandments. The basic thrust of this argument is that a God worthy of worship and obedience must be good, and that without some independent standards of what goodness is human beings would simply have no way to decide whether to follow the commandments of God or the commandments of some evil being like Satan. For example, why was Charles Manson's claim that he was inspired by God rejected out of hand? Answer: Because God (who is good) would never command such things.

This is the most fundamental argument for distinguishing ethics and religion, and is worth mentioning for that reason. Because it is also the most abstract and controversial argument, however, it would lead us too far astray to develop it further here. Instead, we will turn to two more straightforward arguments aimed at showing how, and the extent to which, ethical deliberation and religious belief can (and ought to) be kept distinct.

The first argument is political: An important reason for keeping religion and ethics separate is that the principle of freedom of religion demands it. If religious beliefs are permitted to function as reasons in public disputes about ethics, then a problem immediately arises regarding which particular religious reasons should win out. People holding different religious beliefs, or no religious beliefs, can disagree, and unless one religion is to become "official," the disagreement can be resolved (or lived with) only by appeal to reasons that do not presuppose this or that particular religious view. Although this argument entails that religiously based ethical belief has to be circumscribed by broad political principles, that is, the "public" domain, it preserves a "private" domain within which the personal ethical guidance provided by religious belief is protected. This may be illustrated by distinguishing what is permissible from what is obligatory. For example, although it is permissible for parents to have their children exposed to sex education, it is not therefore obligatory for all parents to do so. Because the majority of parents approve of sex education (consistent with or independent of religious belief), it is often offered as an option in public school curricula.

The second argument is an extension of the first. The argument deriving from freedom of religion has to do with disagreements that are likely to occur between religious groups—for example, between Christian fundamentalists and Jews over school prayer—but disagreements may also occur within religious groups—for example, between Catholics over sex education and birth control. When such disagreements occur it is up to religious leaders to advance and defend their particular interpretations, and it is up to members of religious groups to decide for themselves what positions they will endorse (just as it is up to them to decide what religion they will embrace in the first place). In this way, religious doctrine both has an "open texture" and makes room for conscientious objection, much like the law.

In light of the quasi-legal features of religious doctrine, it cannot in general provide uncontroversial answers to ethical quandaries. In light of the principle of freedom of religion, even when an individual or a group is certain of its conclusions, it does not follow that it may insist that everyone accept the same views. Thus, although no doubt exceedingly important in the "private" (personal) domain, ethical positions grounded exclusively in premises of a particular religion are precluded from the "public" domain of schooling. And, as it turns out, many (if not all) ethical disagreements can be fought out on nonexclusive, "neutral" ethical ground. For example, one needn't endorse this or that religion, or any religion at all, to object to sex education. The grounds might be that it leads to more teen pregnancy; encourages a cavalier attitude toward sex, love, and family; takes time away from the proper function of schools; or is incompetently taught. A host of other reasons might be advanced, each of which, like the above, is independent of religious belief.

References

Bambrough, R. (1963). *The philosophy of Aristotle.* New York: Signet.

Benjamin, M. (1990). *Splitting the difference.* Lawrence: University Press of Kansas.

Benjamin, M., & Curtis, J. (1986). *Ethics in nursing* (2nd ed.). New York: Oxford University Press.

Brown v. *Board of Education*, 347 U.S. 483 (1954).

Bull, B. (1985). Eminence and precocity: An examination of the justification of education for the gifted and talented. *Teachers College Record, 87*(1), 1-19.

Diana v. *Board of Education*, Civil Action No. C-70-37 (N.D. Cal., 1970).

Fischer, L., Schimmel, D., & Kelly, C. (1991). *Teachers and the law* (3rd ed.). New York: Longman.

Gutmann, A. (1987). *Democratic education.* Princeton, NJ: Princeton University Press.

Hampshire, S. (1983). *Morality and conflict.* Cambridge, MA: Harvard University Press.

Hart, H. (1961). *The concept of law.* London: Oxford University Press.

Howe, K. (1985). Two dogmas of educational research. *Educational Researcher, 14*(8), 10-18.

Howe, K. (1986). A conceptual basis for ethics in teacher education. *Journal of Teacher Education, 37*(3), 5-12.

Howe, K. (1989). In defense of outcomes-based conceptions of equal educational opportunity. *Educational Theory, 39*(4), 317-336.

Howe, K. (1990). AIDS education in the public schools: Old wine in new bottles. *Journal of Moral Education, 19*(2), 114-123.

Jonsen, A., & Toulmin, S. (1988). *The abuse of casuistry.* Berkeley: University of California Press.

Larry P. v. *Riles*, 495 F.Supp. 926 (D.C. Cal. 1979), pp. 18, 111, 114, 233.

Lieberman, L. (1985). Special education and regular education: A merger made in heaven? *Exceptional Children, 51*(6), 513-516.

MacIntyre, A. (1981). *After virtue.* Notre Dame, IN: Notre Dame University Press.

Mesinger, J. (1985). Commentary on "A rationale for the merger of special and regular education" or, Is it now time for the lamb to lie down with the lion? *Exceptional Children, 51*(6), 510-512.

Mills v. *Board of Education*, 348 F.Supp. 866 (D.D.C. 1972), pp. 111, 229.

Miramontes, O. (1987). Oral reading miscues of Hispanic students: Implications for assessment of learning disabilities. *Journal of Learning Disabilities*, *20*(10), 627–632.

Miramontes, O. (1990). A comparative study of English oral reading skills in three differently schooled groups of Hispanic students. *Journal of Reading Behavior*, *22*(4), 373–394.

Miramontes, O., & Commins, N. (1991). Redefining literacy and literacy contexts: Discovering a community of learners. In E. Hiebert, Ed., *Literacy for a diverse society: Perspectives, programs and policies* (pp. 75–89). New York: Teachers College Press.

Nagel, T. (1986). *The view from nowhere*. New York: Oxford University Press.

National Commission on Excellence in Education (1983). *A Nation at Risk*. Washington, DC: U.S. Government Printing Office.

Noddings, N. (1984). *Caring: A feminist approach to ethics and moral education*. Berkeley: University of California Press.

Pennsylvania Association for Retarded Children v. *Commonwealth*, 334 F.Supp. 1257 (E.D. Pa. 1971), p. 229.

Reed, S. (1988). Children with AIDS: How schools are responding. *Phi Delta Kappan*, January, K1–K12.

Rowley v. *Board of Education*, 456 U.S. 176 (1982), p. 112.

Salomone, R. (1986). *Equal education under the law*. New York: St. Martins Press.

Shepard, L. (1987). The new push for excellence: Widening the schism between regular and special education. *Exceptional Children*, *53*(4), 327–329.

Stainback, W., & Stainback, S. (1984). A rationale for the merger of special and regular education. *Exceptional Children*, *51*(2), 102–111.

Strahan, R., & Turner, C. (1987). *The courts and the schools*. New York: Longman.

Strike, K., & Soltis, J. (1985). *The ethics of teaching*. New York: Teachers College Press.

Timothy W. v. *Rochester, New Hampshire, School District*, 875 F.2d 954 (1989).

Walzer, M. (1983). *Spheres of justice: A defense of pluralism and equality*. New York: Basic Books.

Index

About the Authors

Kenneth R. Howe is an associate professor in the School of Education, University of Colorado at Boulder, specializing in educational ethics and philosophy and educational research. He has recent publications in the *American Journal of Education*, *Educational Researcher*, *Educational Theory*, *The Journal of Moral Education*, and *The Journal of Special Education*.

Ofelia B. Miramontes is an associate professor in the School of Education, University of Colorado at Boulder, specializing in first and second language acquisition, bilingual special education, and teacher education. She has recent publications in the *American Educational Research Journal*, the *Journal of Special Education*, and the *Journal of Reading Behavior*. She has been director of various special education teacher training projects and a public school regular bilingual and special education teacher.

Printed in the United States
69903LV00002B/1-186

9 780807 731796